BETTER MAN

*An Opportunity to Learn Something from
Someone Who Has Done It All Wrong*

BRUCE LANGDON

Copyright © 2024 Bruce Langdon
All rights reserved
First Edition

Fulton Books
Meadville, PA

Published by Fulton Books 2024

All reasonable attempts have been made to verify the accuracy of the information prohibited in this publication. Nevertheless, the author assumes no responsibility for any errors and/or omissions.

ISBN 979-8-89221-073-7 (paperback)
ISBN 979-8-89221-074-4 (digital)

Printed in the United States of America

The following is a memoir that details my romantic experiences from the time that I began college in 2004 and will focus primarily on three significant relationships between that time and the present day.

I am a gay man who is originally from Atlanta but who resides in North Carolina for the entirety of this **love story**.

Over these years, I earned my bachelor's in psychology, then my master's in mental health counseling. Today, I am a practicing mental health counselor.

I grow up. And I learn some stuff too...

I make plenty of mistakes along the way.

Over the course of this book, I experience love, heartache, good times, turbulent years, and generally the ups-and-downs of life.

And **Taylor Swift** is with me throughout my journey.

To no longer be **haunted** by past decisions, I realized I had to write it all out.

This is my opportunity to speak my truth and hold myself accountable.

With any hope, this book will help someone, somewhere, who is struggling...and perhaps entertain the reader along the way.

CHAPTER 1

Love Story…?

My "before mentality" was this…

I'm a hopeless romantic. (Like, the earliest days of Taylor Swift level hopeless…an unjaded, anything's possible, my-knight-and-**white-horse**-could-be-around-any-corner level hopeless.) I'm in college, which I began at the North Carolina university that fell between the beach and downtown in 2004. Gay marriage didn't have to be legal – I certainly wasn't going to let that stop me from finding my **forever and always** person. He was out there. Meanwhile, I'm bouncing through college, making friends…and dumping guys with a frequency that made my mom say, "Hun…I'm glad you feel comfortable sharing *things* with me and all…but it sounds like you date *a lot* of guys…" That was embarrassing…and I hadn't talked to her about *all* of them, either…

I was going to find Mr. Right in this small, beach adjacent town I called home.

I seemed to have developed an unhealthy habit. I kept labeling guys my 'boyfriend' only to have an a-ha moment ten seconds later: I don't think this is going to work out…

That does not mean the lightbulb went off and we broke up on the spot. Zach and I were together for six whole weeks! And I kinda knew that wasn't going to work before it even got started. But hey, sometimes you've got to date someone who your friends say you won't work out with just to confirm they know what they're talking about.

Jeremy and I made it a couple of months. He was a couple of years older than me. He talked too much about his recent ex-boyfriend's massive penis for me to ever feel super secure in that relationship, and sure enough, they got back together immediately after we split.

Lee was super cute and tall. He was kind of an airhead…I say that, but I'm the airhead who meant to text a friend of mine explaining that I didn't think this Lee-guy was going to work out…which I then accidentally sent to Lee. Whoops. That felt **mean** but was totally a mistake. That effectively broke me up from the only model I ever dated.

Derek was a summer fling, which I guess we both knew from the start. It was still sad to me when he had to go back to Raleigh for school at the end of the summer. And I was pissed when I heard he'd come into town the next weekend and made out with another dude. Ouch!

There was Brian, whose identical twin brother had lost his finger in a milkshake machine at work, and I kid you not, it was served to a customer…We didn't work out because when I was on the phone telling my mom about him, she had questions. That's when I learned that he wasn't in college, he hadn't graduated high school, and – although I don't remember what he said about his GED status, I knew this was going to make Thanksgiving far too challenging if I ever intended on bringing this beau home to Atlanta. But it taught me to be more inquisitive before just trusting a warm fuzzy feeling and running with it.

And so I had an ex named Greg come pick me up and whisk me away from Brian's house. I told him he was my knight-in-shiny-white BMW. We tried to make 'long-distance' work, very briefly. But for college students, the commute between the beach and Raleigh is a hike!

Joey was pretty but it wasn't meant to be.

So I guess it's fair to say my mom wasn't *wrong*…looking back, it's hard to know when I found time for classes. I said to my friend Jayson one day in the car, "I only sleep with people I am exclusively dating." To which J. responded, "Yeah, but you date someone different every two weeks." Sometimes it's good to have your reality checked by those around you.

I was in school for psychology, which I knew from the start was going to mean I'd need to go on for further schooling if I really wanted to do anything with it.

CHAPTER 2

I Knew You Were Trouble

As a young gay man, I was destined to make some bad decisions along the way. Which is why it was nice to have a best friend by my side who made worse decisions. Rob made a lot of "friends" cruising Manhunt. (*That's Grindr over an internet browser, which you would have to click out of very fast any time your manager or a coworker walked by…or else you could get discriminated against and fired! Not to mention cockblocked…*). Rob was a meth dealer with a tendency to disappear for days, barely making it out of the lube coma alive, just to tell his latest trick, "My best friend is coming over. We aren't into each other like that, so you have to go." Then I'd show up with a chocolate milkshake in hand; they were his favorite. I'd pass some exhausted-looking dude with a big smile on his face and Rob and I would hang out.

Rob and I met on the beach one day when I'd gone out there with my friend, Josh. He seemed nice, he was funny, and it was entertaining when we got back to Josh's place and they attempted to break dance. So I was confused when Josh sent me a message on Facebook, stating, "Do not hang out with Rob. He is a walking disease." Well then, why'd you invite him to the beach with us that day, Josh!? Something wasn't adding up. I needed to ask Rob to his face, "Are you a walking disease? And what does that even mean?" Rob and I looked it up. Oh thank goodness! Rob looks nothing like the "walking disease" picture we found on AskJeeves. (* *AskJeeves was kinda like the baby daddy to Google. No one knows where he is today,* *and while they shared similarities, Jeeves is worthless and was never around much.*)

I heard Rob had other friends, he talked about them a lot! Sometimes I'd be over a few days in a row, briefly meeting clients as they dropped in to score. Other times I'd just stop by to say "hey" in between classes. It was nice having a best friend who was cute, gay, had two different-colored eyes, and who cracked me up. We could spoon and it didn't have to mean anything. (Yes, he would change the sheets first).

Apparently, he also knew people - and not just drug clients, either. These allusive friends I kept hearing about seemed to be the people Rob would tell, "I'm kinda busy right now…" when they'd call. But otherwise, he made them sound pretty cool. He always made me laugh and was immensely entertaining. He introduced me to new music, told me about his last break up (that dick!), and explained his mental health issues while showing me his daily pill tray. He told me about his family and his life. He had zero filter when explaining sexual experiences in detail, and specifically talked a lot about a dude's "abs" or "cock" as a big part of what made it worth his time or not. I remember asking him where "face" and "smile" fell on the list for him, poking fun. They were on there, too…somewhere. He used to say random things, like "hot diggity dog on a lickety-split bun" when something got him excited. He was fucking hilarious.

Eventually, after we'd fallen deep into platonic love with each other, Rob finally admitted to something. "I've been keeping you from meeting my friends intentionally because I've wanted to keep you all to myself." What an amazingly sweet, undeniably creepy, possessive-in-all-the-best-ways thing to say! He'd clinched my heart… and he could pinch the shit out of you with his toes, so watch out.

And then I finally met his friends. Trey, Matt, Joe, "Chicken Little" (who had been my waiter at Chili's and who was hella cute), Randy, Brantley, Brantley's partner Barton Fields (who was at least in his fifties, and that's probably being generous). There was a whole cast of characters, and that was just the beginning.

I also met Rob's ex, having heard about him for quite a while. Rob was about twenty-three at this stage of the story, just being a few years older than me. Rob's ex was Jean. He was in his early forties. I could see that, sure, he was handsome…for an old guy. But all I'd heard aside from that was Rob's report of what a jerk he'd been, especially at the end of the relationship when he pretty much "abandoned" Rob. I think they were together a couple of years before Jean up and vanished. He was seemingly standoffish with Rob…standoffish but willing to be in the same space at least. I'm not sure how long he'd been gone, or how long he'd been back. I later learned that he'd been gone long enough to be certain Rob knew it was over and had calmed down, whatever that meant. As far as I could tell, Rob had been plenty stable since I'd met him. What were these people alluding to? I did not know. And I wasn't trying to get wrapped up in gossip, or pry.

There was also Jon, who owned the nightclub downtown. He was Jean's best friend, and he was in his early forties as well. I'd been out to this nightclub a handful of times before meeting Rob, as you didn't have to be twenty-one to get in. It was always a fun time, hanging out with friends, watching drag shows, rubbing the x's off your hands so you could drink (cigarette ashes took those x's right off! And at this time, you could still smoke in the club!)…typical college stuff. The difference between going in with Rob versus going in with my friends from college was that Rob walked in with the keys to the kingdom. He'd show me places in the club I didn't know existed, places I figured we would get kicked out for being in – the DJ booth (nope, he's not a DJ any more than I am…) and the third floor where drag queens changed and the offices were located. As much fun as the tour was, there wasn't a dance floor up on this 3rd floor, and that's where I wanted to be, most always. Fortunately, Rob liked to dance too. Ya see? I knew I made a good choice!…(in what?) In my best friend.

Now that Rob had introduced me to some of his friends, I was no longer left speculating who these imaginary friends he'd been speaking of actually were. (I was no longer on **the outside**.) Rob's ex had previously just been 'Jean, who reportedly has a big dick and kisses like a parrot.' Now there was a face to the name. And 'Jon, the nightclub owner godfather of downtown gays' now had a face as well.

The first time I met Jon, like any true gentleman does, he offered me a line of cocaine in his garage-attached office. So yeah, super nice guy. Not to mention he smoked my brand of cigarettes! Now, I was nineteen or twenty at the time, and my best friend from home (Britt) liked to harp on this idea that "there are cooler ways to die [than from cigarettes]." So I knew smoking wasn't cool, but check it out, here this dude's like forty-four-ish (maybe?), and in his infinite wisdom, he knows to go for Marlboro Lights as well. Epic. He's not dead, so by my estimation, I've got about twenty to twenty-five years to amass a fortune so I too can smoke cigarettes in a detached garage apartment where my office is located with a pool house and pool out back, two white fluffy dogs, and a historical house located in downtown. Jon's **big reputation** was something people talked about, at least partially because he had **nice things.**

Good cocaine in NC was notoriously non-existent. Being from Atlanta and having done more cocaine in high school than most do in a lifetime, I knew good cocaine. I was pleasantly surprised that Jon hadn't tricked me into baby powdering my nose; he actually had good cocaine. A mid-forties white guy who isn't closet smoking or hiding it from anybody? With good cocaine and who is at least mildly entertaining in the brief exchanges we've had. "Man!" I remember thinking, "I wish my dad was this cool."

Later that evening, up in the third floor office at the club, Rob and I went up to check in with Jon. Again…moving away from the dance floor…but silly me for not understanding…we get in there, and it's GHB time! The half-filled cranberry juice cups with no ice had left the bartender looking puzzled but now things were making more sense. Jon was crunching numbers in the office behind the desk, but he cut that nonsense out and began pouring something into the cups with Rob's assistance. Not long after that, I found myself sitting in Jon's lap, just chillin'. Fully clothed, of course. To my knowledge, GHB did not make you think people were Santa Claus. I definitely didn't know Jon well enough to think that's where I belonged. So how I got there I don't really know. But the three of us were just chatting and laughing. There were other people coming in and out of the room, as well, like the manager of the bar and anyone else who needed something from the office. It was fun! I knew GHB had a "date-rape-drug" label, but I also knew it was described as "liquid ecstasy" by others, it just depended on the dose you took and whether you took it willingly and knowingly that made the distinction. So while no one would pop a roofie by choice, GHB was a different story.

Later and away from the office, Rob pulled me aside and said, "Hey…Jon is off limits. Okay?" Rob was calling dibs, I guess? I hadn't even thought of Jon "like that", so yes, of course. At this point, I had dated dudes that were exclusively in my own check boxes — skinny/slim (check), white (check), and my age or as many as a whole two years older. And there were plenty of guys to choose from in this college town! I'd been trying to keep an open mind about Rob being with his ex Jean and all the heartbreak that caused him, but the ageist inside of me didn't get it. And I wasn't getting this latest Jon development either. In my head I was thinking, "Wait, doesn't Jon have a boyfriend anyway? And wouldn't you getting with Jon be weird since Jon is Jean's best friend?" But all that came out of my mouth was, "Yeah, of course…" I let it be known I was not a threat, because after all, "…he's old." It hadn't really crossed my mind that Jon being flirty needed additional intervention, but I guess Rob had his sights set on Jon (and I did not), so…let the games begin(!?). Because, as I mentioned, Jon did have a live-in boyfriend named Mark. Or, so I'd heard… I guess even though Mark hadn't been around Jon any of the times since I'd met Jon, apparently he did exist. And if Mark wasn't a deterrent for Rob at that time, I figured it was none of my business.

CHAPTER 3

The Story of Us

Remember how I mentioned Jon had a live-in boyfriend, Mark? Yeah, not anymore. Jon had "fallen asleep" in the pool house when Rob was staying back there. Apparently, Mark had been "furious." Well, yeah, that's understandable. Monogamy was the norm, even in gay relationships, and this was a deal-breaker for that relationship (apparently). That's all I heard about what went down. But it seemed Mark was out, and Rob was in, the boyfriend spot, that is. I don't remember when Rob moved in or if he just never left after Mark was gone. But I don't remember going back to Rob's apartment after that time…at least not the original one…

So that was that.

I remember words once said by a wise man named Erik Blitzen. Those words being "Jon Carter is incapable of being alone." I think the sentiment behind the words was probably, "Jon Carter always has a boyfriend. I've never known him to be alone." I'm only speculating what Erik meant by that because I cannot ask him directly. Erik passed away from cancer. He was a great dude, and this isn't the last time we'll hear from him in this **story of us…**

Remember when I mentioned that I was a hopeless romantic? The only thing I could define I was looking for in a partner at that time was that I just wanted to be with someone who inspired me to be a better person. You know, the type of person who motivates positivity and growth and all of that in another human. Someone who, just by being themselves, makes you makes you want to be better. I'm in my Taylor Swift world, and settling for anything less just seemed silly, because he was out there.

My perception of my own **reputation** at this point in time was for being "always friendly" and "always happy." I was known for my smile and more than that for "always smiling." I was definitely a positive person. To illustrate, one summer I was working at a hotel on the beach as a front desk person, checking guests in and making sure they had a great stay with us, etc. Well, I walked over to the restaurant to get some coffee and got to talking with some of the waitresses that were working at the time. One of them dropped a basket of sweetener packets, so I was helping her and another girl pick them up. Then I walked to the other side of this half-wall where the coffee pots were to make the coffee I'd come for in the first place. I was out of sight, doing my thing, when waitress #1 said to her colleague, "Do you think he is ALWAYS in that good of a mood? No one can always be that nice…" When I came back around the wall she turned bright red, flustered, and admitted, "Oh my gosh, I thought you'd gone back to the desk, I didn't mean any—" I just cut her off and said, "Hey, if that's the worst thing people are saying about me behind my back, I am totally okay with that." I smiled and went back to the desk. I thought it was funny.

And I just wanted to share that clip so no one got it twisted. I wanted to be with a person who inspired me to be the best version of myself. Looking for a **Romeo**, his **white horse**, all that good stuff. After all, I'm an **ever lovely jewel**…(right?)…now let's do this thing! But where was he?

CHAPTER 4

Sparks Fly

> **All I can say is it was enchanting**
> **to meet you...**
> **This night is sparkling, don't you let it go**
> **I'm wonderstruck, blushing all the way home**
> **I'll spend forever wondering if you**
> **knew I was enchanted to meet you.**
> **-Enchanted**, Taylor Swift

It's funny to me that the very first time I hung out with Kris McRay included us walking along the sidewalks in the downtown area, by the river, as the sun came up. More fitting lyrics for how I felt do not exist.

> **I don't wanna look at anything else now that**
> **I saw you**
> **I don't wanna think of anything else now that**
> **I thought of you...**
> **Now I see daylight.**
> **-Daylight**, Taylor Swift

Before I spell it out fully, Kris was my **paper rings**. He was my **love story** – but without all of the bullshit leading up to Romeo realizing what he had and what he could lose. Kris treated me like he knew from the minute we met.

He's also pretty clever. He was a choreography teacher. We had just met and were getting to know each other. He was showing me some of the dance videos on his phone. We were sitting on my couch as he scrolled from one dance photo to the next, when, oops!, what was that? Yep, there was a dick pic right in the middle of the media he intended for me to see. This was a _very_ effective marketing technique. He later admitted he knew that pic was there, even though at the time he played it off like it was so embarrassing. Well played, Mr. McRay. Well played.

From the minute we met we were pretty much inseparable.

Oh yeah, remember how I said he was a choreographer? I can't tell you how many times we **moved the furniture so we could dance...**

I thought I knew how to dance to Britney Spears's choreography like a boss...Kris showed me what it looked like as a pro.

And the best thing about this man? He did inspire me in all the ways I'd been looking for. He was genuine, kind, caring, compassionate – and not just towards me, towards people. He was great then, and he is great now.

I was just looking over Facebook records to get a more concrete idea of when certain events occurred, and the wall posts I used to send this man were nauseating. They're the type of posts that make me think, "I just threw up in my mouth a little...that is SO gay."

Sadly I came up in a time when saying something is "gay" was a regularly hurled insult among adolescents. Even sadder? Present day, it still is. I think to a lesser degree, but like I mentioned, I'm a therapist. I have adolescent clients. The straight clients have confirmed that yes, some people still say this as an insult. And my LGBT+ clients have confirmed that yes, it is still hurtful. The encouraging thing, however, is that both groups — straight and gay (/queer) adolescents, alike — have all confirmed a common theme: it is only the dumb kids that still use homophobic language. So, as sad as it to hear that this language is still used in a derogatory manner, with proper parenting and kids gaining awareness about this fact, my hope is that we can irradicate bigoted language, altogether, across the board. Afterall, what parent wants their kid to be the *last idiot on the playground? And what kid wants to inadvertently label themselves a moron?

-Spread the word-

I just took my own childhood trauma and turned it into a PSA. Also...

PS - When I said my own Facebook posts to Kris McCray are "gay," I'm allowed to do that. They're literally posts to my boyfriend about how much I love him. And what could be gayer than that?

I strongly encourage everyone to cue up the **"You Need to Calm Down"** music video right now and recognize how much fun gay people are. I'm not trying to hate on straights, y'all are capable of having fun, too. But I'll take Pride parades over any other type of parade, any day. I'll take circuit parties over raves (although I'd rather just go to both, so don't make me choose, please). And I'll take gay nightclubs over straight bars any day of the week.

Wow...that was a tangent.

Readers: As for the barfing I mentioned, I'm gonna make y'all do it too. But before I go there, let me say this: I hope everyone experiences a love like Kris in their lifetime. Because everyone deserves to feel special, appreciated, beautiful, sexy, awesome, amazing, lucky... and for any religious people, *blessed*. Yes, even you, Republicans.

Alright, everybody, you got your airplane bag ready? (Am I showing my age by asking that? Privilege? Do any airlines have them anymore...? Hmmm...)

Facebook message from Kris (August 23, 2007):

> Bruce Bruce Bruce, boy am i in trouble. i just dont see how something like this can be real!! you are the most beautiful person inside and out! im sorry if i acted funny sometimes, but i mean i just dont understand how something this great can be true. i know we were talkin each others ear off this morning, but it felt so good to share feelings with someone again, and know that the person i was to was listen and care about what i was talking about. you said some things that made me really look @

you and say WOW i know this could work!! i have been thinkin the whole time to myself "god i hope this can work or i want this to work". But after last night, i know YOU & I could be happy for a LONG time to come. when you were talkin about your grand dad and how he prays at diner!! the way you talked about two people being in love, that was something real! something i have have seen and i think people our age dont care about but you do. so do i. people like you and me are a dime a dozen! i want a love like that, i thought it would never happen til i heard to talkin and was like wow there is someone else out there. i know it doesnt happen over night, and im not tryin to rush anything. which brings me to the key, that was so sweet and cute when you were tryin to give me your key, but baby I know your doin alot of big steps with me that you never taken before, and that is great but dont feel like you have to. i promise im not goin anywhere. i honestly wanna lay down with you every night and wake up with you everyday. you have made me question how i felt about guys before cuz I have never felt like this and i dont know how to act, im use to the uncomfortable feeling, now that im comfortable its kinda scary but im started to really like IT!! anyway just wanted to share that with you. I love you!! your home now from class YAY!! i get hugs and kisses!!

Kris

Facebook response to Kris (August 24, 2007):

hey there Kris Langray McDon!!-
I'm sitting in my den right now at 11:43 PM as you sleep soundly in my bed because I

can't sleep and on top of that Baiju just called me so she's not doing anything to help the sleeping situation. I'm not happy about this cuz, as you know, I have class bright and early tomorrow morning plus my mom's getting into town and DAMNIT, I need to get some sleep! But since I'm awake anyway and you're hopefully busy having sweet dreams, I'm going to take this opportunity to respond to your e-mail. 1st of all, to be honest, when I first read it I got nervous and a lil uncomfortable because I don't wanna jinks anything. Things have been going so great, which I'm very very happy about, and I guess I'm just not used to that when I'm dating someone so I don't know what to think! You are sooo great and so sweet and the feelings I have for you are so strong that when I read your e-mail that all kinda hit me at 1nce and it was overwhelming. I do feel the same way you do though! I don't wanna say "I could see this lasting a LONG time" cuz I'm a lil superstitious and silly, but I know I definitely could see the same thing. I'm glad what I said about my grandparents had an effect on you because that's how I really feel and a lot of times my own relationships and the relationships of my gay friends make me feel hopeless about the possibility of "happily ever after" with just 1 guy. That's ultimately what I want and I pray that someday I can say I truly have loved someone the way my grandparents love each other. I'll be a very lucky guy if that works out the way I hope it does!! Changing topics slightly, I can't believe ur about to meet my mom! I'm not gonna lie, it makes me nervous! I'm not nervous because I don't think she'll like you or anything like that at all, it's because I just know how badly I want her to see what I see in you and be happy for me ☺ I think she will, but still, I can't help that it's runnin' thru my mind. Anyway, that's all I really got 4 now, so I'm end by saying I LOVE YOU!!!! and hope you're having sweet sweet dreams baby ☺ Ur the best! XOXOXO.

Love love love,
Bruce

PS-I may run over to Comfort Suites to give Baiju my school schedule now cuz that's what she asked me to do in the message she just left. I'll be back ASAP tho and u can call me, of course, if u wake up. "These words are my own, from my heart flow…I love you, I love you, I love you, I love you!" ☺

If you remember the man with the wise words from earlier in the story, Erik Blitzen…he was Kris's roommate when we first started dating. Mykah, Erik's long-term boyfriend, and a couple of other guys also lived there. ("Long term" in the gay world when I was twenty-one meant three or more years…) Mykah and Erik were defying all odds, by my count. They were record breakers in that department. And on top of that, from where I was sitting, they were stupid in love. They were overtly into each other, and not in a gross way. In an adorable-nickname-PDA-lucky-to-have-found-you kind of way. (Previously defined as the I-just-threw-up-in-my-mouth-a-little kind of way.) So Erik was there to witness our relationship as it began. And so it meant something when he told Kris he could tell we had something special. "Y'all look like Mykah and I did when we first got together."

Some of the highlights were things like when Kris decorated my apartment for my birthday with streamers and balloons to surprise me when I got home from work or class as a surprise. It was a surprise and it was very sweet. Balloons all over the floor. I hugged him, then

I stepped outside the door and told him after I closed it I needed him to pop all of the balloons because I hate the idea of sitting in a room where any of them could pop unexpectedly at any minute. He was so fucking sweet (and he didn't know how I felt about balloons!). He certainly got credit for this move, as sometimes it is 100 percent the thought that counts!! And the streamers stayed up. Lol.

This one made me feel really special…

Kris explained after we got together that dance moms and other teachers alike had been commenting about how their daughters' lyrical dance numbers that he was teaching them for competitions had really been impressive lately. And no lie, these girls were phenomenal. One of the cutest things about Kris was how excited he got just talking about how good they each were and how connected he was with their parents (the moms, really). Each of his students had a solo they'd perform that he'd choreographed and they'd learned and practiced over some number of weeks until it was time for their competitions. Kris would mix the music himself; he was also ridiculously talented in that department. I'd heard enough of the music he was making to know generally what was going on. Plus, I'd visit him at the studio when he was working sometimes to see the magic happening firsthand. His girls were incredibly talented. I didn't know much about lyrical dance, but I didn't have to – I could tell that they were top notch. (People with dance experience also remarked that they were *a leap above*, so that is not just me being biased!) "Love Song" by P!nk, "The Special Two" by Missy Higgins. "I Wanna Grow Old with You" by Westlife (*this song still makes me cry). "I love you" by Kina. There was a group number about kissing that spanned *The Little Mermaid* and closed with Cher belting "The Shoop Shoop Song (It's in His Kiss)." There's a little taste, to get an idea of what kind of music Mr. McRay was using. Alicia Keys was in there, too. Leona Lewis. Celine Dion. It was intense.

To be told I was the inspiration for lyrical dance numbers that come together for competition and all of the songs are about love. *That* was a lot. But it was beautiful. And magical. And I never want to forget feeling like anything's possible, with The Power of Love…

(and that wasn't even the Celine song he picked. *Hint: 'cause baby I taste you, feel you, breathe you, need you...*)

Whether it makes you barf or your heart explodes, I just know I feel lightheaded remembering what it's like to be *that* in love.

(Sidenote: Erik realized that "The Special Two" is about infidelity. But Kris edited it to keep it on-brand. He was not about to put something in the show that was love *adjacent*. And it is an awesome song.)

Kris and I got together when I was 21 and he was 25. It's an understatement to describe him as "creative"; he can also draw and paint. In fact, he paint-penned the lid to my apartment's toilet seat and even that was amazing. Some people are just talented beyond belief and he is truly the most creative person I have known in this lifetime, to this day.

We got along well. We met each other's families. We came from different backgrounds, but that made me love him even more. As we were planning our first trip to Atlanta for a family event on my mother's side, he was so nervous. He had been asking Erik all about what order to use silverware in at a country club. It was so cute to me how much he cared. I'd simply informed him that my mom was a nightmare but only behind closed doors with her closest friends and family. I assured him that she'd be sweet as can be around him, no worries, and that even when speaking to me privately she had better be nice if she knew what was good for her. I had his back and he had mine.

When it comes to moms, Kris has the best of the best. Present day: Mama Joan quit smoking over a year ago now, and I am so proud of her. She's the type of person we ALL need on this Earth forever because she brings the level of goodness up, exponentially. She's tough, sarcastic, sweet and sassy. She won't put up with any bullshit. I have no doubt most of Kris's best qualities came from her, through nature and nurture. She was a single mom to Kris. They adore each other. And she loves me, to this day. She "played" mom to all of Kris's friends. She knew how much I loved her son and how much he loved me.

And now Kris was gearing up to spend time around my mother. Yikes.

In the house I grew up in, and the mom I grew up with was incredibly gossipy. She used to tell her kids and her gossipy friends all of the dirt going on within the Buckhead community. For example, when my younger brother and I were kids and our high-school-aged babysitter was watching us, my brother looked up at him and blurted out, "My mom says your mom's an alcoholic!" I was just enough older than my little brother to know better than to repeat my mom's "disclosures." It was around this time that I began developing some code of ethics to live by including specific morals and values, which came to include this principle: I try to never say things behind people's backs unless I've already said it to the person's face. After all, if someone doesn't know they have room for improvement, how can they improve? And saying it behind someone's back just robs them of the chance to do something about it, not to mention it's a bad look for the person doing the talking.

The harder the truth to tell, the truer the friend who tells it.

I couldn't stop my mom from going on her gossipy power walks with a friend, talking about kids and parents from the snooty private school I attended. But I can strive to be better and learn from her mistakes…right?

But back to Kris and our first visit to Atlanta…

> **There we are again in the middle of the night**
> **We're dancing 'round the kitchen in the refrigerator light**
> **Down the stairs…**
>
> -All Too Well, Taylor Swift

Whoops! Kris and I took some GHB up in my bedroom at my mom's house in Atlanta, and my dumb ass felt like I needed to go downstairs and dance around the kitchen in the refrigerator light… naked. Fortunately, Kris was able to wrangle me back upstairs before my mom and stepdad were awakened. They are very heavy sleepers and I am grateful for that. Their bedroom door opens up to the stairs

I was twirling (...or should I say swirling...) down. This could've been incredibly embarrassing, and I was not being quiet. So thank you, Kris!

This also happened, during the day. *Call it **All Too Well** (Bruce's Version)?

> My told you me
> **~~Your~~ mother's ~~tellin'~~ stories 'bout ~~you~~ on the tee-ball team**
> **You taught me 'bout your past thinking your future was me**

Kris and my mother got along great. Kris got along with everyone in my family, and all of my friends, wonderfully. He's an easy person to get along with.

My mom shared with Kris and me that she had recently been in Ireland with her husband (/my stepdad) Tom at a costume party. She had dressed up as Tinkerbell. Kris later told me he felt like she would've made a badass Ursula ("those poor unfortunate souls" Ursula). I got mad at him; after all, that was my mom! (Although in retrospect I'm sure his assessment of her costume choice was at least in part reflected in all the stressful things I'd said about her.) Kris was quick to insist this was not meant as an insult! He explained that plenty of drag queens dress up as Ursula. Kris questioned (*changing from his own voice to his best Ursula impression at the end*), "can't you see your mom, in costume, talking about *BODY LANGUAGE?*..."

When we later relayed Kris's assessment to my dad (her former husband), he thought it was pretty fucking funny.

> **You think that it's funny when**
> **I'm mad, mad, mad**
> **But I think that it's best if we both stay**
> -***Stay, Stay, Stay***, Taylor Swift

CHAPTER 5

Road Trip

Jon had a big DJ coming to play at the club, and as such he'd put in a big order with a dealer in Columbia, SC for some ecstasy. Being the helpful team players that we are, Kris and I agreed to go make the pick-up since Jon was too busy preparing for the festivities. From my residence to Columbia was a three-hour trek. I knew the route well, as Columbia was about the halfway point on my trips home to Atlanta. Kris and I had both met Brad, the guy we were picking up from, in previous expeditions we'd taken with Rob. And so we set out on our quest.

We were about an hour from Brad's house when my Acura SUV literally caught on fire underneath. We pulled off the road and started making calls, both to Brad to see how we could get to him as well as to car repair places. We also called Jon to give him the unfortunate update. Eventually it worked out that the car was towed away, and someone picked us up and took us to Brad's house. Now, we just had to figure out how the hell we were getting back home with all these pills.

Luckily, Brad had a friend at the house who was willing to drive us home. We had obviously lost time and needed to figure things out. I don't think we were able to leave until the next morning, but at least we had transportation. So we got into this man's little red Honda and headed back on our three-hour journey. As we rode, our driver just started talking…and talking…and talking. He was going into detail about how he really shouldn't be driving, given that he did not have a license…and given that the tags on the car were either non-existent or expired…and that with the warrants out for his arrest, if we got pulled over, the car would definitely be getting searched, and he'd definitely be going to jail. This was the most stressful ride I'd had in the back seat of a car, to date.

Fortunately, we did make it back home, although I believe we missed the DJ and afterparty altogether. I was just glad we hadn't gotten pulled over, and to have Kris there provided some additional comfort. I don't remember how or if we were compensated for our troubles, I think all I really wanted was to go to sleep at that point.

My mom ended up spending $4,000 to have the transmission in that Acura MDX replaced, after which I resumed driving it for a couple of months. Jon needed an SUV for his power tools since he did various work at the night club, the hotel, as well as rental properties. So he bought the car a couple of months later. I didn't necessarily need an SUV and gas prices were going up, so it seemed to make sense. It wasn't until after my mom greenlighted the sale for $2,000 that she remembered how much she'd spent on the transmission. But she made a point to call and let me know whenever that lightbulb moment occurred to her.

CHAPTER 6

Anti-Hero

According to an online age calculator, when I initially posted "I LOVE YOU" on Kris's Facebook page, I was twenty-one years, eight months, two weeks and five days old. We'll round up in just a second.

Kris was a great guy. And still is, to this day.

I wasn't always such a great boyfriend. I felt justified in being critical, always with the mentality that I knew I was coming from a good place in terms of the spirit behind the message. I am quite certain, in retrospect, that my upbringing and being raised with a different concept of money influenced how I felt things should play out. Things like, "Why don't you have a car? You should…since you're always using mine…" Things like that. (I knew cars didn't just fall from the sky, that would be dangerous. Or grow on trees, whatever the appropriate saying is.) Kris worked *hard* for what he had. (Haha, that made me giggle.) Did I mention his…

Passion?
Energy?
Nine?
Inches?
Style? LOL. I got "dickstracted."

Oh wait, let's go check on our other cast of characters!

CHAPTER 7

New Romantics

Rob had been living downtown at Jon's estate during the time Kris and I were living uptown. We still hung out — Rob and me, that is. After all, a best friend is a best friend. I'll admit, I think we both did some degree of that thing you do in a new relationship where you forget you have friends because being around your person just feels like where you belong. But since Jon owned the nightclub downtown and I was in school uptown, weekends made sense for hangout time. And I loved going out. After parties at Jon's house were always a fun time, not to mention walkable distance to and from the club. Major changes worth noting: Rob quit dealing meth. He'd been working the front desk at a hotel up Market Street. (With Baiju! Initially his manager, then our manager, then my manager…then neither of our managers. Rob would work the overnight shift, rearrange a bunch of stuff to be "helpful", then she couldn't find anything, and I'd hear all about it from her throughout my shift. So even when Rob and I didn't get to hang out, I got to hear his name out of her mouth, so it was almost like he was there.)

I don't know a whole lot of what was going on between Rob and Jon, but that's their story to tell anyway. They didn't seem unhappy… from Rob's reports, things were pretty good. They would go on trips, and upon return, Rob would show me pics of the two of them in hot tubs looking happy. Jon was a busy guy. He had businesses to go and do things for. Rob was mostly at the house when he wasn't working (I think). Sometimes he'd want to hang out but was a bit more reclusive than he had been. Part of me just figured this was meth-free Rob. (Like, in *Friends,* Fun Bobby on the sauce versus off. Similar situation? Perhaps.) Rob would still go out to the club; after all, Jon was pretty much there every weekend, being the owner and all. The third floor still didn't have a dance floor; but I'd spend time up there, less begrudgingly, since it had become a bit trickier to get Rob to come downstairs. I got the sense that it was not Jon insisting Rob stay by his side so much as Rob feeling more antisocial (Jon-attached). He was still funny but less jovial. He seemed to have a bit of a superiority thing going on, not with me so much as when he'd interact with other people. Plus, he would talk about the club's employees needing to up their game, in a way that was different than any comments he'd previously made. But I was in my own little world, boppin' to the beat of my own drum. I had lots of friends at the club, so I still got plenty of time running around. Things were fine. I figured.

If something was off, it was easier just to assume that this is just Rob's new temperament because he wasn't high on meth all the time. It wasn't like an are-you-sure-you're-okay level difference, but it was a difference.

Also, before even moving in with Jon, Rob told me he'd been diagnosed with bipolar. As I went further in my education it crossed my mind that borderline personality disorder felt like a better fit. But whatever the diagnosis for my friend was, at twenty-one I couldn't do anything to predict or to prevent him from ending up with the head trauma that was on the horizon…

CHAPTER 8

Til Ya Come back home...

Kris was making dance magic. **We were happy**. I'd probably become a bit less of a pink-cloud warrior than I once was. I'd be like, "Babe, you need your own car. Because when we fight and I need space, I need to be able to make you go to your apartment without having to drive you over there." (Like, ya know, cuz cars are cheap and all. So…just go get one…right?) He drove my car more than I did. The dance studio was further away than my walk to class, so that made sense for him to have it. I had two legs. And if I was going to need it at some point, I'd just drop him off to work and I'd have the car. "Kris must have his own vehicle" may very well have been me creating a problem where there was none. After all, this was disaster prep for the hypothetical fight we may get into someday. At this stage in the game, I pretty much wanted him around all the time…and waking up next to him was the best part of every day.

*Suggested listen: "**22**" by **Taylor Swift.** In case anyone can't remember what it's like to be this age, you should give it a listen. But no pressure. She captures twenty-two perfectly.

CHAPTER 9

Click, Click, Boom!

But speaking of cars, I will say one thing that drove me nuts now that I mention it. Kris didn't wear his seat belt...ever. And this is what I mean by I always knew I had good intentions. My underlying message here, of course, was, "I don't want anything bad to happen to you ever because I love you." But here's how that may look over time when it's every time you get in the car and your partner never buckles up...

"Don't forget to buckle up! (*Click*.)
"Hey, babe, seat belt! (*Click*.)
"I'm not going anywhere until you do one thing. What is that one thing? (Eye roll. *Click*.)
"You don't wear your seatbelt, ever, when I'm not here to remind you...do you? (*Click*.) Me: "I love you..."
Waiting...then, "You know I don't want anything bad to happen to you, right? (Wait for it...wait. Light bulb! *Click*.)
"What do you think it'd feel like, your face going through a windshield...? (*Click*. Eye roll.)
"If next time we get in the car, you put your seatbelt on right away, I'll give you head." (Eye roll.)
~*Click*.
~*Click*.
~*Click*.
~*Click*.

I can't take credit for putting that genius idea into practice. I didn't have it until just now. Pavlov would be so proud. I'll never know if it would have been an effective intervention…?

In reality, only those first five examples happened and were recycled. But I do remember thinking that if I could get him to always buckle up, whether I was there or not, then I'd have made what I considered to be a positive impact on him. Plus, I wouldn't have to worry as much about his safety or a ticket or whatever. He made me a **better man**. Surely I could return the favor…

CHAPTER 10

You Know She Writes All Her Own Music, Right?

Things are going to get sad, scary, and stupid. Hearts get broken. Heads get busted. But before we get into all of that...

...On a lighter note...

Jon texted me and encouraged me to get Rob to come hang out... out of the house...because Jon needed space (but I guess couldn't ask directly?). So I swung by and picked him up. Rob and I ran around town, just jamming to the new **Fearless** CD as we went. And when that one had played all the way through, thank goodness I had her original album, **Taylor Swift**, also. Rob mostly listened to club music but also Janis Joplin, Alanis Morissette, and maybe sometimes gay porn, playing softly in the background. But I could tell that songs like **"I'm Only Me When I'm with You"** and **"Fifteen"** really had him reflecting on how much he valued our friendship. I was right there with him, thinking the same thing. He even asked, "Hey, who is this bitch?" at one point, to which I explained she was Taylor Swift, she's a miracle, and she writes her own music. I can't believe I haven't told you about her already! When we got back to Jon's house and went inside, Jon was like, "Back so soon?" to which Rob replied, "Oh my god, I had to get out of that car! He won't stop making me listen to this Taylor Swift chick! He's trying to torture me with teardrops on guitars and friendship songs!" I laughed so fucking hard. Then I looked at Jon and said, "You know, she writes all her own music."

CHAPTER 11

...A Thousand Cuts (minus the death part)

I wouldn't be trying to tell someone else's story, but I have to… at least from my own perspective and memory bank. It becomes relevant down the road. If the timeline gets jumbled, it's only because it's not totally my lived experience, I was more of a sideline character… until I wasn't. **Are you ready for it?…**

Rob and Jon went on a trip to Thailand. When they got back, they came with gifts for Kris and me. We were excited to hear how the trip had gone. Well…we thought we were…

Let's just say it wasn't the trip either of them had hoped it would be. Rob had contracted MRSA, and the Thai doctors had removed a sizable cantaloupe scoop of a chunk from his calf. It was gross-looking. Rob had a lot to say about Jon's overseas drug use, speaking quite unfavorably about his fiendish use of a drug called Yabba (which I had never heard of. They described it as being crack-adjacent). Jon reported even before the MRSA, Rob and he couldn't get on the same page as to what they wanted to do from day to day. Kris and I listened to what seemed, from my perspective, to be a competition to prove who most effectively ruined the trip with them each one-upping the other. So…yeah…Kris and I thanked them for the T-shirts and exited stage left. They weren't fighting the moment we left, per se, but it seemed there was some **bad blood.**

And then…

Rob moved out of Jon's house downtown. They may have briefly broken up, and that's why he moved out, maybe. But they didn't stay broken up. I was at their house one time that I remember where they were shouting about each other to me, "No, look at the crazy look in *his* eye!" "No, you're the crazy looking one. Look at *your* eyes!" I'm not sure where the fight had started, and I also wasn't sure if I was supposed to make a judgment call as to who "crazy eyes" actually was. But to me, they were both acting crazy.

Things were clearly becoming more turbulent.

My recollection is that there was an incident for which the police were called. I remember Jon telling me the story of having to chat with an officer, but by the time the officer had gotten there Rob had calmed down, leaving Jon feeling like he looked like the "crazy one.")

You make me crazier…crazier…

And there was an incident where Rob ran full speed at the pool house door, which was glass, head down, and shattered it. It makes sense that this was all one incident, but I think it was two separate ones. All Rob told me about his head-butting the door was, "I needed Jon to feel the pain I was in."

I'm not sure if any of these triggered the move out or if it was some other event or development. I think this is when Rob moved in with a dude named Mike, although that also may be out of order. Again, not my story to tell, and not my memory to hold. It is relevant to know that Rob moved out, though…

I say that their breakup didn't last because, as Jon explained it at the time, "I break up with him, and then when I wake up the next morning, he's in my bed."

CHAPTER 12

The Moment I Knew

I would also nag Kris about his teeth, specifically, about getting the two back ones that were missing replaced. They didn't bother me, but I was often wondering what other people were thinking about them, first impressions, etc. (This was very much tied in with a Buckhead upbringing, where everyone got braces and had straight white teeth before leaving high school, if not middle school.) When I initially talked to Kris about getting his teeth "fixed", he stated issues with teeth generally run in his family. I'm guessing the fact that he pretty much survived on Coca-Cola wasn't helping the situation… but I digress. It didn't change the fact that I loved his smile, but I figured as a dance teacher interacting with parents so much, having your teeth look their best made sense. I don't know why I felt the need to bring this up, ever (and I wish I hadn't). I certainly had no connection at the time with how expensive dental work is, and that having braces (twice) as a kid and yearly dental check-ins isn't everyone's experience.

I wasn't a complete dick about it either. I've never been mean to Kris, why would anyone be? But trying to change your partner implies there's something wrong with them, and in reality, he was everything I'd wanted in a partner.

I'm sure another piece to it was my own nerves around his meeting my family. Wait, let's be real — my mom. When "Did you hear who's having a baby out of wedlock?" or "[Insert name]'s mother's breath smells like wine, before communion, every week…" are just typical conversations she's having with you or with people around you, you just come to realize no one is safe. She just likes to gossip, and I was protective of Kris. It's irritating to think I was concerned that when Kris and I left an Atlanta visit, my mom could be asking my sister, "Did you see those teeth?" I'm sure in this hypothetical my sister would have just rolled her eyes. Because she loved Kris. And to be fair, I never caught wind of my mom running her mouth about him, although no one would've called me up to blast her like that anyway, most people have a healthy fear of her and know better. (Except me, I guess…type, type, typing my death sentence at this moment…LOL).

Disclaimer: I need to give credit where credit is due here. This is a summary of how I viewed my mom, at this time in my life. Today, she's not actually this way. I didn't speak to her for five years, and I mailed her a DBT workbook that I later was told she completed. Coming to the end of year three of the silent treatment, I told myself — to myself — that if ever six months went by where none of my family members or others told me problematic things my mom had done or said, I'd speak to her again. So if you're doing the math, then yes, there were a few more incidents. But when I realized it had been six months – and I was high on pain meds following an eye surgery – I called her out of the blue. But anyway, twenty-two-year-old me would've thrown her under the bus and gotten back to the story, but today I have to recognize that she did some work, or something shifted in her and she deserves credit. So that's my "**punished-you-with-silence**" to "**speak now**" story with my mother.

But back to me, nagging Kris. Teeth…Car…You need to have your own apartment and go there sometimes. When were these times, I'm not sure. I think he was just supposed to figure out that I needed space before I even realized it or something. And while none of these conversations were fights, telling him how to spend his money on what I saw as self-improvement items was not cool. And while these weren't everyday conversations or anything, over time I'm sure they had an impact on him negatively, especially when efforts he made either backfired (like when he bought a car that broke down quickly and to pay the repairs would've overshadowed what he'd paid for the car) or just felt like a slow progression forward. (Teeth — he went to the dentist; don't get me wrong. If I remember correctly the dental work he'd needed done was not inexpensive, but they'd come up with a plan: pay-as-we-go kind of thing. I believe one of the dance moms was the dentist, in fact, so it was less than it would be. But without insurance, that's still not cheap.)

While I didn't necessarily feel I was nagging him in the moment and as these conversations were happening, at some point it dawned on me that he was different. We were coming up on two years together. He was kind of detached seeming. He didn't smile as much or as brightly. He just kind of existed in the same space as me. He didn't get excited about other people much either. He didn't talk about what he was doing at the dance studio; he wasn't mixing music or hanging out with many people. I think he would still draw some, but he wasn't eager to show it off or proud of what he was doing, as far as I could tell. I decided, without discussing with him much about my observations, that I had single-handedly killed his spirit. This amazingly talented, excited, and enthusiastic individual had his internal spark extinguished by me, his boyfriend, over time. It wasn't something I had to convince myself of, I just had this idea that that's what had happened, and I decided it was an absolute fact. And I felt horrible about it. My idea of what my ideal partner would be was simply someone who would inspire me to be better, and I had robbed this person I loved so much of that same gift. The idea of being a negative influence on him was not something I could live with and not do something about. And he'd been in this funk for a couple of months when it registered with me. So I knew what had to happen. I had to set him free. I would never want to drag someone down and I hated that I hadn't seen it sooner.

> **Never wanted this, never wanna see you hurt**
> **Every little bump in the road, I tried to swerve...**
> -**Breathe**, Taylor Swift

My first ever excruciatingly hard relationship conversation in this lifetime was that day on my couch with Kris McRay.

It hurt me to see him hurt. And I'd convinced myself I was the reason. I'd decided that the resounding message of "You're not good enough" because he wasn't making money and putting it toward getting his teeth fixed or toward having a functional car had beat him down.

I let him know I loved him and I always would, but feeling like I'd sent this amazing person into depression's depths, we just weren't good for each other anymore…

> **It's me, hi**
> **I'm the problem, it's me.**
>   -**Anti-Hero,** Taylor Swift

*Suggested listen: **Last Kiss** -Taylor Swift

Sometime over the next couple of weeks, Kris and I met up to talk. He came over to my apartment, and that's when he told me he'd been taking a lot more opiate pain medication than I was aware of. That was where the money went that caused the halt of any dental work, car repair, or going out and doing things with his friends. He didn't say anything about goals to change that, necessarily, but at least I had some insight into the change I'd noticed in him. I still felt like my nagging contributed, whether to his mood change or his addiction. So, for better or worse, it was over, over. He offered to stay and cuddle but I told him if we cuddled, I'd never want him to leave. Maybe I should've said yes…but I'd never broken up with someone and then gone back on it. And relationships that are on-and-off are never healthy. I just knew I needed space to figure me out…

I hope everyone gets at least one great love in their lifetime. This man used to let me know about the change his boss and the dance moms noted in his work and his attitude when he and I started dating. I knew I brought him up, he told me, all the time, in lots of different ways. And when I saw his girls (students) perform at competitions, I was blown away by their talent, which reflected his talent, which I'd supposedly influenced. Like I said, I hope everyone has a great love in this lifetime. I know who mine was.

> **I wish I could fly**
> **I'd pick you up and we'd go back in time**
> **I'd write this in the sky**
> **I miss you like it was the very first night.**
> -**The Very First Night**, Taylor Swift

Unfortunately, things had to get really bad between us before they got…neutral.

So I spent some time flying solo and processing this breakup. I remember walking out of art class (remember, I'm in college) with a few friends and just mentioning my recent ex-boyfriend (I'm sure if I was leaving art class, I was probably talking about how talented he was or something, even if I was supposed to be getting over it). One of the girls I was walking with asked, "Can I see a picture of him?" So I pulled one up on Facebook where we are smiling, all cuddled up. Her comment was, "Well, clearly you were the cuter one in the relationship." I just wanted to punch her in the face. (I think there's a Carrie Bradshaw breakup rule about picture destruction that applies here…he looked sexy to me.)

Tangent: When you're trying to support a friend through an emotional breakup, "There are plenty of fish in the sea," or "You were the cuter one in the relationship" or "The best way to get over him is to get under someone else" (even if there's some truth to that one), none of these are what your friend wants to hear if they cared about the other person. All well-intentioned, no doubt! But still… (and no, she has no idea that comment ruffled my feathers. I know she meant well). *Note: I could start listing what not to say to comfort a friend who lost a loved one, but that feels too far off course.*

Anyway…

I'd been single for a couple of months. Kris and I were going about this breakup the way that I felt like I had to, which is no contact. (The goal being: **I forgot that you existed**…even though you never really will. Once you've healed, it'll be better. But for now…).

I wasn't really entertaining the idea of getting back together; but I had a strong sense that if I saw him, hugged him, talked to him, messaged with him, looked at pictures of him, whatever, I'd fall into it so quickly. And I wasn't trying to find myself **trying to change your mind once you're already flying through the free-fall**. I figured healing from a really significant relationship must include getting over the idea that you and he are still meant to be, and that that goes away, eventually…right? So I was waiting…waiting…waiting… That feeling wasn't extinguishing…but I thought about him less. Until I'd be around Rob and he'd bring him up.

Speaking of Rob…

Rob and Kris became roommates. Dust between Kris and me settled, even if my brain was struggling to get there. When I want to hang out with Rob it pretty much just isn't at his place unless Kris is at work or otherwise away. Rob and Jon are together-ish.

I don't know if there's a psychological term for what I'm about to say, but if there is not, it should be something like Opposite but Proportionate Emotions. What I'm talking about is the concept that the degree to which you feel one emotion is proportionate to the degree to which you will reflexively feel its opposite emotion if things flip. If you are extremely excited about something, you will be proportionately devastated if it doesn't work out. If you love someone with every fiber of your being, that person can absolutely shatter you to your core. Hate, rage, or reducing you to a puddle — all are on the table as possibilities.

Anybody else **wonderin' why we bother with love if it never lasts?**

I didn't know if Kris and I could figure things out down the road. I'd kind of thought he was my **forever and always**, but what to do about that I wasn't sure…I just felt like to figure that out I really couldn't see him for a while or speak to him or message him.

*Suggested listen: **You're on Your Own, Kid** -Taylor Swift

So I spent that summer **tryin' to be my old self again, but I'm still trying to find it**. I had the summer…the whole, long, **cruel summer**… — about three and a half months — to feel normal again. And I was starting to. After all, summers in this beach side town were a fun time. Inevitably this no-contact situation wasn't going to last forever; we had too many of the same people, places, and things in common. I was intentional…or should I say hypervigilant…about avoiding a chance encounter. Honestly, I think I was scared I'd see him again and he'd be "Kris on pills" and it would totally kill the hope I had. Of course, if I saw him and he was himself, I'd fall back into it so hard…and I had a secondary fear that he'd be himself, we'd be back together, and then I'd just sink his mood again. Or something would. But the concern that I would sink his mood was much greater than it would be something else. (**Anti-hero** thinking.)

CHAPTER 13

You Might Think I'm Bulletproof, but I'm Not

Left my 'bookbag' **there, at** 'our mutual friends' **house**…

Facebook message from Kris (May 6, 2009):

Meredith Grey really got to me last week on *Grey's*. All her talk about fighting for someone. When we broke up i layed in bed everything night and went through all the stupid shit i made you deal with. and all i could think was why didnt i just walk away or leave and let it blow over. all i could think about was all the bad times, and i started tellin myself i need to start moving on. i've been dumped before, but this was different. then we talked and you broke down and everything changed. all this time i was trippin and acting stupid because i didnt think you loved me like i loved you. but after that talk, all i thought then was about all the good times we had, and just the memories made me believe it could be good even great again. i know you dont want us to be a couple you have told yourself it will never work, and you're right, with an attitude like that nothing would work. i really thought you'd be the last person i would ever be with, and i have never thought that about anyone before. my heart is telling me to fight for you, to do whatever needs to be done. Relationships go through tough times, and getting through them makes the relationship strong. im not sayin we have to jump into anything right now, or anything but dont write US off because your scarred, my heart just wont let go of you, my mind tells me you're gonna find everything wrong cuz you are affaired of being hurt. Bruce if you truely believe in the depths of your heart and soul we'll never work, and you honestly believe that not because you are tryin to make yourself believe that but because you do, that there is nothing there at all left for you to try to flight for, then ill never say another word about it and we'll be friends, but i just dont believe that you truely believe that. not after you sayin you dont want me to stay and cuddle because you'll never want me to leave. i think you're scared let go, and you arent willing to fight for us.

dont worry you havent lead me on and our friendship will be great if that's the final outcome. Even hooking up doesnt bother me, hell i'd almost stay single forever just to make sure i can still have sex with you, you so sexy like janet:) i havent told you in awhile, but i love you, i really do.

Love Kris

*Suggested listen: **The Way I Loved You** -Taylor Swift

Kris and I had managed to cross paths minimally if at all since breaking up. Messages were minimal, but Facebook did save that one (above). I did not respond. I'm quite certain that if I had, I could have saved myself from literally the most agonizing feeling of…ever.

I went over to Rob and Kris's house to hang out with Rob, and I was finally going to go over without first asking if Kris would be there. Intentionally. Leaving it up to fate. I think I may've told Rob to let Kris know I'd be coming so he could decide if he wanted to see me before I was just in his space. So maybe not totally leaving it up to fate. I just didn't want to inflict myself on him if he wasn't in the headspace. And so we saw each other in person, and wouldn't you know it. All of the butterflies I was hoping were dead suddenly came back to life. Fuck. In my mind, this is a blank spot. How much we spoke or what we talked about is blank. (Literal **blank space**.) What I remember is the feelings being reignited. I'm sure I had secondary thoughts and feelings about that, but I just knew I loved this guy the same way I had since, honestly, the day we met. And yes, he was himself. Which was probably all I needed to verify before my heart was essentially back in his hands. How long I was there, how long we talked, what about, whether Rob was there, all of it is a blank, today. I'm guessing Rob and I went out downtown or something from there, and Rob drove. This is my guess because otherwise, I wouldn't have left my bookbag with my laptop in it there in the living room. In all likelihood, that had been the plan all along. Come over, let's go out later! But what the plans were that night, plans I participated in making at the time, none of it stuck in my memory bank because all I could think of was that I was going to be in the same space as Kris. And it felt good. Flirting in person or over text were not things I had done in a long time. We talked about the possibility of hanging out and just seeing where "we" were. While I don't have a memory of this part, Facebook exchanges back up that he'd suggested I come over the next night to watch a movie that was scheduled to air at 8:00 p.m. I don't remember committing to these plans, but like I said, I don't remember much of what we discussed. I just remember the feelings.

So I'd be lying if I didn't say I was pretty excited about the potential of seeing where things would go with Kris. I absolutely missed him. I thought perhaps whatever issues he'd attributed to pills had subsided. He had seemed more like his old self again. But this was feeling more and more like I'd rushed to judgment and assumed I was the problem when his behaviors really did align with what I knew about opiate use. *Specifically, physical symptoms…ya know, the kind that can affect whether or not you believe your partner is still into you…[Hint: "It's NOT that common, it DOESN'T happen to every guy, and it IS a big deal!" (-Rachel, Friends)]. But anyway…that was a one-time thing.*

The day after I'd been hanging out with Rob and had seen Kris at their place, I needed to get my bookbag back. Being that I was still in college, this mattered.

The only problem with me getting it back was that Rob was at work, so he couldn't help. "Call Kris. He'll let you in." Yeah, of course he would…Rob said he should be home. So I texted him, initially, pretty much as I was driving over there. He didn't respond, so I called when I got closer. Still nothing. Rob said he'd be home. I was already almost there. I'm sure I could knock hard enough to wake him up if I had to…

Since my calls went unanswered and I needed my bookbag, I figured, I could face Kris without a buffer (Rob). This is fine…

So I started knocking and waiting and knocking. Finally, the door opened and there was Kris, pretty much naked. And sweaty. And smiling…he just mentioned something about, "Uh, Max Long is over here…uh…what's up…?" I'm direct quoting when, in all fairness, all I really remember is a name being muttered somewhere in there. I think I managed to tell him I needed my bookbag. He closed the door, got the bookbag, and brought it to me. I got back in my car. I think I made it around the corner before I started ugly crying like you would not believe. Like, hyperventilating, hysterical, you-should-not-be-driving-type crying.

I didn't know what to do. Rob was at work so he couldn't help. And Kris was who I'd want to call if anyone…so I called Jon.

Now, Jon hung out with Rob's friends, but almost exclusively when Rob was at work and with the understanding that it would upset Rob to find out. Since their relationship had gotten rocky, why rock the boat for Rob anymore?

But, yeah, so in my tears-flooding-the-car moment, I called Jon. I do not think he could understand most of what I said, but he got the gist and said, "Just come over." So I did.

> **How can a person know everything at eighteen**
> **But nothing at twenty-two?**
> -**Nothing New**, Taylor Swift

CHAPTER 14

I Did Something Bad

Arriving at Jon's house, I was embarrassed. This man was my employer at the time, but also a friend. And I had just ugly cried over the phone over a boy who I felt like I was getting over-but-then-back-into feelings with. And Jon knew my side of the breakup with Kris, not because I'm particularly chatty about my personal life (*until fifteen years later, apparently*) but because Jon is inquisitive. Like, I used to call him "The Quizmaster" level inquisitive.

And I could venture to speculate he knew Kris's side of it as well. I can't be totally sure, but I do know that when Rob had been at work, Jon had gone over to Kris's to hang out with him and a mutual friend named Keeley. Again, I can't be certain, and it really doesn't matter now, but the idea that he wouldn't have asked Kris about the breakup at some point is almost unfathomable.

The Quizmaster: Jon asked his friend, Barton Fields, who is a mass-scale pig farmer, so many questions about operations that Barton apparently thought Jon was gunning to try and start his own mass-scale pig business, according to Jon. (I wasn't there for this conversation. Jon just told me about it. So yeah, Jon asks a lot of questions. Always.)

It wasn't especially odd for me to be at Jon's house during the day, but it wasn't something that happened regularly. Any other time I'd been over when Rob wasn't around was because I had picked something up for Jon during a recent trip home to Atlanta. Jon had his reasons for keeping what I was bringing him a secret from Rob…

Flashback: Sometime in late 2008, I'd estimate, Jon picked my brain about whether I could find meth when I was home for the holidays. I told him I'd see what I could figure out while I was in Atlanta and keep him posted. While in Atlanta, I dragged a couple of my straight, non-meth-using friends to a sketchy bar on Cheshire Bridge, and wouldn't you know it? The very first person I asked hooked me up with his friend's contact info. That's how I met Marcus, the meth dealer (and hair stylist!). I immediately alerted Jon that I had, in fact, found a source. Jon wired me money, and suddenly I was transporting an ounce or two between Atlanta and North Carolina. Atlanta was the meth capital of the south at the time. Jon informed me when I brought that first package to his house that the prices he was paying in North Carolina were steep. I hadn't realized prior to this conversation that Jon pretty much always had meth.

I didn't go home to Atlanta very often, but this was not an isolated event. But it was the first time I'd ever been responsible for that much of someone else's money (or that much meth, for that matter.). A couple of the times Jon had me stop by and pick up cash as I was leaving for a trip home. This actually made me much more nervous than transporting the meth ever did. I wondered what I would say if the money ever got stolen and I had to try and explain why I was returning empty-handed. Fortunately, this never happened.

And so, the times I'd been at Jon's house in the middle of the day when Rob wasn't there had been to drop off Jon's package. Jon and I would hang out in his office for half an hour, maybe. Rob lived in Jon's house at the time of those early deliveries. And even if Rob was stuck at work, I couldn't stick around at Jon's for long. I wanted to get back to my side of town and back to Kris. Of course, that had all changed…And on this day, my now ex, Kris, had shattered my heart.

The embarrassment around expressing so much emotion over the phone when I called Jon that day was because I had not seen this man emote before; we didn't know each other like that. In fact, while working at his hotel, he made a point to show me jokingly that his brother Tommy was buckled into the passenger seat of Jon's car. In an urn. After he had recently died and been cremated. Jon chuckled about this to several people, eventually moving Tommy to the trunk. In all fairness, "Captain Crazy" (a.k.a. Tommy) probably would have appreciated getting a few more laughs and odd looks from the people Jon showed, as Tommy was very funny. But back to the story…

So I walked myself and my tearstained face into Jon's house and into his office (which had been moved inside since the beginning of this story). Fortunately, Jon, like his (dead) brother, is a very funny person and helped me in that moment to laugh about being so emotional rather than judge myself. So maybe calling him wasn't the worst idea…? We were chatting about things, both Kris-related and not, Rob-related and not, other people. Jon offered me some GHB. Um, yes…absolutely. As I mentioned earlier, they call it liquid ecstasy for a reason – and who's ever been sad on ecstasy? Not me… so we kept chatting. Jon inquired about another friend. "Chicken Little" was his nickname. Oh, you mean Chris Wiggam? Or Chris Whigman? I couldn't remember his last name exactly, but I knew who Jon was asking about. Jon pulled up Facebook and started trying to find him…no success…

I'm not certain why we needed to find him — if this was a Jon-driven quest or if he'd sparked my curiosity too. But I ended up typing in the search box while sitting in Jon's lap. "Found him!" And would you believe it? We then had sex.

So yes, **I did something bad.**

CHAPTER 15

Haunted

The problem with sleeping with your best friend's on-again-off-again-but-sure-at-this-moment-ex-boyfriend is that you don't feel good about yourself. It doesn't matter if you're alone or if you're around your best friend or if you're around anybody. You always just kind of know that you're not actually as good of a person as you believed you were before it happened. It's not even so much of a thought you're having as it is an unshakeable feeling. (*Predictable and poorly timed as it may be...*) You can't just **shake it off.**

We all three hung out one final time, all three meaning Jon, Rob, and me. (Rob and I hung out together other times, just not with Jon). Jon had gotten some ketamine — Rob's favorite! I don't know how I got the invite or whatever, but I came over as Rob was baking it up. We all snorted a big line and were sprawled out on Jon's orange fluffy rug. (This rug sounds like it would be heinous with the description...it wasn't. Maybe peach would be a better descriptor... it doesn't matter.) I remember Jon's foot grazing mine, and he kind of smiled at me. Playing footsy can be cute, but not when you're in the room with your questionably stable best friend who is still hung up on this guy, even if the guy insists they're done. But ketamine allows everyone to be pretty much too out of it to be too mad about much of anything. Also, Rob didn't see, and it did not continue.

Things continued as normal with Rob believing he and Jon could work things out and Jon not wanting to work it out but not wanting to trigger Rob into any kind of episode. Jon and I didn't have any conversation about sleeping together the one time, at least not that I can recall. We also weren't planning to do it again. The one time was kind of like any other time I'd been around Jon that Rob wasn't going to benefit from knowing about. Anything Jon did with a friend of Rob's…well, aside from sleeping with me…could be viewed as Jon looking out for Rob, in a way. Like when he hung out with Kris and Keeley at Kris and Rob's apartment when Rob was at work. They were both close friends of Rob's, so I have no doubt Jon checked in with them both about Rob's mental health. Jon had a tendency to want outside perspectives on Rob while also sharing his own updates. Perhaps it was an overshare that he didn't want to be with Rob anymore, but didn't know how to make a breakup stick without upsetting Rob…but that was common knowledge and had been for a while. I both understood why it was tricky to figure out while also not having the voice to say to Jon, "Since Rob moved out, he seems more like himself." And he did. He certainly wasn't head-butting doors. Maybe just not living on the property somehow was helpful, I'm not sure. I just know he was back to joking more and seemed like his mood had lifted a bit.

I know from being close to Rob his perspective on certain things. That day when Rob and I drove around listening to Taylor Swift, Rob complained about Jon never coming to his apartment and not seeming to want to. I guess Rob thought his boyfriend should want to see where he was living and make some of the effort for them to spend time together.

A friend of mine named Dennis came into town. He had previously lived in the area but had moved away. We met at my apartment, then drove downtown to go out for the evening. We met up with Rob at the club and had a standard evening out. It became clear that Dennis and Rob were flirting, so I was not surprised when Rob told me he was taking Dennis home with him. That worked for me, so I headed back to my apartment.

Jon had been ducking Rob in all sorts of elaborate ways, like parking his car away from the house so he wouldn't know Jon was home and other such maneuvers. While it was odd to me how much Jon would do just to avoid Rob, I didn't really question it. But when

Jon learned that Rob was taking someone home with him, he wanted to hear all about it, so he came over to my apartment with his questions about Dennis and the situation. As Jon and I were talking, suddenly someone pounded on my door. It was a bit of a shock to see Rob was **on the other side of the** peephole. At the time I couldn't register why he would be there, and it didn't dawn on me until reliving this story that I'm sure he was bringing Dennis back to his car. But when Rob discovered Jon's car in my apartment parking lot he wanted to know what was up. Jon hid, briefly. Rob asked why Jon's car was there. I'm sure I was not making much sense, and that's when Jon stepped out. We were fully clothed because we were not hooking up and had only been talking. But still, I was his best friend, Jon was his "ex ish" boyfriend, and we didn't have to be hooking up for it to feel like a stab in the back.

CHAPTER 16

Better Man

It's fair to say that from the start, getting into a relationship with Jon was not going to make me a better man, if for no other reason than the circumstances under which we got together. Jon had been looking for an exit strategy from Rob for quite some time. He didn't want to have to do what Jean had done and just disappear from town, indefinitely, but he had thought about it. (I know this because he told me.) Jon invited me over a couple of times when I was getting off work, only to have Rob show up at the house. This was not a comfortable time, as I'd be stuck in the bedroom while Jon had intercepted Rob at the back door, explaining that no he couldn't come in, no there wasn't anyone there, he just didn't want Rob there. I could hear Rob saying things like, "I don't care about being friends with *him*. I just don't want to lose a friendship with *you!*"

Looking back, I wish I had said "no" to those invites now; and even if this is just hindsight, had I known Rob would show up, I absolutely would have declined the invitation. I did enjoy Jon's company, but I wasn't trying to create drama. An additional complicating factor is that saying "no" would've meant saying "no" to my employer, given that he owned the hotel where I'd just gotten off work. In a perfect world, I would have already had after-work plans because I am a particularly terrible liar. Instead, I went along with the complications of leaving my car at the hotel and Jon driving us back to his house… which didn't work since Rob would show up just wanting to see Jon anyway. So instead we'd stay at the hotel or my apartment. Jon had been playing the park-my-car-elsewhere-so-Rob-doesn't-know-I'm-home game for a while. So when Jon was already at the hotel doing work, I got roped into the game too. It was not a fun game.

Looking back on it now, it feels more like I was there to unknowingly ensure Jon wouldn't cave on the breakup. It wasn't my intention, but I was getting some insight into what Jon meant when he said the thing about breaking things off and then the next day waking up to Rob in his bed. If I hadn't been in the bedroom, I'd imagine Jon would have just said, "Well…alright. Come on in, I guess…"

This felt really shitty.

When you burn down a best friendship, you almost feel like you have to make it into something worthwhile. At least that's what I thought at the time, like, turn this into a significant something or else you're without a best friend, a partner, or a Kris.

My stance toward the situation shifted a bit. Jon continued to say to me that he and Rob were done and that he just needed to do all he could to maintain Rob's sanity. I was working at a hospital in Jacksonville at the time, driving about an hour to work a twelve hour shift, then coming back. Jon had both Rob and Kris doing work for him to make some cash, which Jon kept insisting he was doing simply to keep the peace with Rob, almost insinuating that he was worried about his own safety in the situation. I didn't become aggravated about this until Jon told me that in the club bathroom stall with Rob, while the two were smoking meth, Rob pulled Jon's penis out while Jon was hitting the pipe. Wait…what? *For anyone who doesn't have a dick, unzipping someone's shorts and pulling out their dick would take enough time to where you could stop the person before your dick is actually out, even with a meth pipe in your mouth.* I don't have any idea how Jon reacted at this moment, as I was not there, or what impression Rob was left with. But Jon had acted like he needed help getting out of the Rob relationship, and yet he's not stopping Rob from doing something like this? It made no sense to me. Rob didn't have to see Jon's dick to maintain his sanity, I was quite sure of that much. So Jon's whole spending-time-with-Rob-begrudgingly-to-monitor-his-sanity claim quit holding water for me…

I was twenty-three and Jon was forty-seven. I'd have to imagine some of my ageist ideas had subsided over the time I'd been around the people in this story. And now Jon and I had slept together. Not to mention I'd ruined a friendship. Jon didn't get why him maintaining a friendship with Rob didn't sit well with me, even after Rob pulled Jon's dick out. In my mind, it was because Jon hadn't stopped him when he went to do it more than anything else; otherwise, I wouldn't have cared so much.

So what's so great about Jon?

Well, he's funny. People like him. He's friendly. And it's undeniable that for the town where we lived— especially in the gay community — he's kind of a big deal.

He's undeniably interesting. If you're his partner, you can hold his attention long enough to learn so much about him. I've heard his entire work history, his dating history, highlights from his life story, all about his family. It's always been interesting to me to hear all about a person, from Jon's perspective, and then meet them myself and get to put a face to the name.

Highlights from his dating history were especially interesting, as I heard his side of how the relationship had been, as he'd experienced it, and then would later meet these former boyfriends when they'd stop through town for a visit.

One of the former partners I got to meet, "A," has a mother who is a nurse and who worked at a hospital where I was also working. We only had one shift on the same unit, but when she realized that I knew Jon, her face changed. She was super nice to me, but I could tell there was a lot she wanted to say. I never got to work with her again, but if I had, I would like to think she would have dropped the filter. I could tell she wanted to. Again, I have no idea what she would've said...

Someone I did get to hear from more directly was his ex AJ. Everything I'd ever heard about AJ from Jon had been benign. Jon said AJ watched The Weather Channel a lot. And I think it was Jon's brother who had described AJ as Jon's "little joey," like a kangaroo's offspring. Jon said that he had broken up with AJ but didn't give any details at the time. But besides those points, I didn't have much of a backstory, at least not this early in the relationship. But AJ was coming to town with his boyfriend, and we were going to be meeting them out for drinks.

All was well as we greeted AJ and his partner. He and Jon looked happy to see one another. AJ was cute and friendly. He was noticeably younger than Jon, but I wasn't passing judgment (obviously), it was just an observation. It is simply worth noting because of the exes I'd now encountered, Mark had been younger than Jon but not quite as significantly as myself or Rob.

At some point during our time at the bar, I was chatting with AJ and Jon was not paying us any attention. I was on my second drink so I'm only guessing here, but I think AJ was as well when AJ started telling me things about Jon and about their relationship. AJ sounded resentful, noting that they'd been strung out on cocaine when things ended and that the only way AJ managed to get out of there was because it was time to go to college.

Plenty of people have a couple of drinks and **make fun of our exes**, but this felt different. AJ knew I was dating Jon, so to this day, I don't know if he was just saying these things because he was tipsy or if he was letting me know, "Blink twice if you need help escaping," or some other nudge. He did make it clear that life after Jon had been much better for him and that he was happy. (Since AJ didn't know Jon was supplying me with a steady stream of meth, surely he couldn't have predicted how the story was landing as he told it to me…could he?)

So what did my dumb ass do?

I talked to Jon about it once we were back at his house, of course! When I mentioned AJ possibly not having the highest opinion of him, his initial reaction was, "Sure he does! I'm friends with all of my exes!" (Except Mitchell. I don't know the backstory there, but apparently this guy dumped Jon, and it devastated him. That's all I know, and I have never met him.) When Jon learned that AJ had said something negative, his defenses went up. Suddenly AJ wasn't just the weather-watching joey he had been before; he became the coke-addicted ex who begged to stay with Jon who had desperately pounded on Jon's door to be let back in after Jon had thrown him out.

Two wildly different accounts. And who knows where the truth lies? But if AJ had been trying to alert me to the light on the other side, I was not ready to see it. I felt like having this conversation with Jon was necessary because I didn't want to be keeping secrets and out of some sense of loyalty to Jon. I really liked AJ a lot, so my intent was not to throw him under the bus but to get some clarity around why Jon's report of AJ had initially been fairly neutral while AJ's report of Jon had not been so favorable.

Jon had a very different perspective than I did on a lot of things, which kept things interesting. Being into psychology and speaking with someone who seems normal but perceives the world and people in it so differently than I did kept me on my toes, to say the least. For example, the idea that "people are going to treat you differently once they know we're together" encouraged me to question the motives of others in a way that my brain still doesn't quite vibe with. I've been well-liked for almost all of my life, so the idea that I needed to start doubting people's sincerity because of who my boyfriend was, that was a bit of a mind fuck. But anyway…onto his…

CHAPTER 17

Big Reputation

Dating someone with a **big reputation**, you'd think **would be a big conversation…**

And I can't lie, there were things **I heard about** him (**you**) that didn't always paint him in the best of lights, let's just say. But I was willing to overlook that and give this a shot.

As an example, when Erik from earlier in the story mentioned the thing about Jon being incapable of being alone. I brought that statement up to Jon early on to see if there was any truth to it, from his perspective. (No secrets in a new relationship, right?) Jon's response side stepped the point completely as he began explaining how he'd had to fire Mykah for stealing from the bar. I guess Jon was insinuating that Erik was running his mouth because he was bitter that Mykah had been fired since Mykah was Erik's boyfriend(?). (And to be clear, Mykah's "theft" wasn't him putting wads of cash into his pockets or anything, it was something about drinks being wrung into the cash register in a way that looked suspicious.) All I knew was that from Mark to Rob to me there had been no "alone time"…and Erik had made this statement before Jon and I were even friends, really. But I felt like I was keeping my conscience clear by letting Jon know the things I'd heard about him.

Prior to getting to know him personally, I knew some basics: He owned the gay nightclub downtown and he was known to have fun after-parties at his house by the pool, typically after the club closed.

And he likes younger guys (younger than himself was how I interpreted that at the time).

Working at his hotel, I saw firsthand that he's a power-tool-wielding gay, not the fruitier variety. He's super hardworking and was typically smiling when he'd show up at the hotel to fix something, *unless* the person behind the front desk was wearing his club clothes from the night before and not his uniform. That caused his smile to fade quickly and got me yelled at, so I knew I'd fucked up. *Side note: I'd woken up somewhere on his property, probably the pool house, that morning just in time for work and would have been late had I rushed uptown to my apartment before work to change! But no excuses...I'm sure I'm misquoting very slightly here, but the sentiment was, "What the fuck are you doing behind my front desk in a T-shirt!?" It's funny to me now, but at that moment, seeing his face go from zero to pissed in an instant when, at this time, he was my employer — definitely not my boyfriend and probably not quite a friend just yet — was scary. But he went from pissed to calm almost equally as quickly...*

Jon and I met when I was an undergrad, somewhere between age nineteen and twenty. I had graduated but was not yet back in grad school when we got together. I moved in with him in November of 2010, officially, after the threat of Rob subsided, but we essentially spent every night together, it just wasn't ever at the same place. We would stay in a vacant room at the Coral View Hotel that he owned or at my apartment, primarily because he wasn't feeling like he could be at his house due to the Rob factor. I was more than okay with this, as I did not want another night like we'd had the couple of times we had unexpected company.

One of the times he was over before I sublet my apartment, he excitedly elbowed me in the mouth. It was a reflexive jerk moment and completely unintentional. I think we were watching something on an iPad or a phone. It was not a big thing, but he insisted I go check in the bathroom mirror, and sure enough my tooth was chipped – one of the front four on top. I wasn't mad. I went to the dentist a couple of times to try and get it fixed, but the piece they put in to fill it kept falling out when I'd eat certain things. But oh well, having perfect teeth was overrated.

When I sublet my apartment, illegally, it was to a lovely couple who was very pleased there would be no background check to hold things up. And I moved downtown.

CHAPTER 18

When Someone Tells You Who They Are, Believe Them

In the early days of our relationship, Jon provided information, jokingly, about how he had been in past relationships. Things I should have probably paid more attention to. Things like…

"When I'm done with a relationship, let's just say I have a tendency to stop trying."

"I've been known to try to get the other person to break up with me."

At the time, he and I were happy. So whatever follow-up questions I now wished I'd asked did not come. (Like, "What the fuck exactly does that mean!?" would have been a good one to ask, retrospectively.) But instead, I laughed along with him.

Other similar tidbits he provided? "When a relationship is really done, you can count on me to come back to try and reignite what's been burned to the ground" or some similar sentiment.

Again, he was referring to past relationship experiences he'd had when he said it. He seemed to be poking fun at himself and recalling the evidence that supported these sentiments, internally. He laughed, and so did I. Again, at this point in time **we were happy**.

He also mentioned that you know a couple is in trouble when they don't travel together, but he was speaking about another couple we knew, not necessarily remembering anything from his own past, I don't think.

I used to pick on Jon early on. He was regularly running his mouth about someone…or should I say everyone. I pointed out to him his shit-talking ways and let him know I did not think it was cute. One of his favorite lines was, "If you don't have anything nice to say, come sit next to me." We were having a conversation about this in the shower. I remember light heartedly bringing this up, explaining that when I'm around him 24-7 and I see firsthand that he talks shit about everyone I'm left wondering what he says about me?…

He took offense to the idea that he talked shit about *everyone.*

I responded simply by blurting out the name of one of his closest friends, to which he replied, "Well, he is pretty boring."

We both laughed really hard. And to his credit, I think he did talk *less* shit, moving forward (at least in my presence). (Although it is also possible that I became desensitized to it…perhaps a little of both. But hey, compromise is the key to healthy relationships, right?)

I felt loved in this relationship because I was "pretty sure" he didn't talk shit about me to others. Also, because him talking less shit about his friends and employees at my request meant he cared about me, somehow. It's twisted, but this did make me feel special.

On the flip side of shit-talking was that Jon never gave anyone a compliment. I mean, working at the hotel, no one got one. At the bar, certainly not. I pointed this out to him. I also noted how quick he was to let someone know if they were underperforming or doing something wrong. Since I originally brought this to his attention in a lighthearted way, something like, "Oh, right, because we both know how much you *love* giving compliments and all", Jon responded with, "Well, if people would just do things worth giving compliments for it wouldn't be such a problem." Bringing this up more directly results in responses like, "I give compliments, I give them all the time. You don't know what you're talking about." But since we were still happy at this time, it wasn't something I pressed. (These were my very intentional attempts at forcing Jon to be what I saw as a "better man" — don't talk shit, give compliments, generally spread kindness…teaching an old dog new tricks = exhausting.)

About employees, Jon was very much of the belief that "if they're not stealing a little, they're stealing a lot" (a sentiment voiced in *The Grifters*, 1990).

If one were to point out to Jon that he never admits to being wrong (again) it's all in *how* you bring it up and the spirit behind it that determines how he's going to respond. He used to joke, "I'd admit it if ever it happens" or "Well, lucky for me, I'm never wrong." This was cute, and we laughed about it. I didn't need him to be wrong…but if ever the day came where he was, I had hoped he'd be able to see it and say it. (Note to self: Don't hold your breath.)

All these observations are based on being around Jon as much as I was. I wasn't personally affected by any of this *initially*, it was more observing these traits in him and between him and other people.

But when it became clear that some of these ways of being did impact dynamics between us, there were times when it could be quite infuriating. We actually broke up early on…and based on these emails I'm not sure why it didn't stick…

This email came after I got mad when Jon shared that Rob had managed to "pull my dick out" in the club bathroom stall:

*E-mail titled "**dear John**" from Jon to Bruce. Aug 24, 2010 (7AM).*

Bruce,

GOOD MORNING. I'm not sure how the wheels came off the track last night but whatever the reason I think it's pretty clear there are issues that go beyond rob that are causing problems. Rob is just a fuse. I'll take my share of responsibility for the current state of affairs. I have been a little unsettled for a while over some things between us that I was hoping would work them self's out over time and I'm sure that hasn't helped. I do love u and now is probably a good place to start working on a friendship before we let a misfiltted committed but tainted relationship tear us up beyond repair. So we can be friends, fuck buddies, or something in between but let's both try and respect each other. My gun is back in its holster.

            Jonny

I responded that evening (at 6:42p.m.)...

  Isn't this e-mail a little redundant? I mean, most of this has been said, and is where we both knew we stood. The only thing I'd change is I'm taking fuck buddies off the table, as that's borderline disrespectful to even suggest, but I'm gonna let that slide for the sake of our friendship. We don't need to discuss what went wrong any further, and I'm gonna try to forget that u went through my phone, and know that there are things about you that I love being around that make you a good friend and a fun person, and try to forget any character flaws that caused a relationship to be impossible. No more dissecting a relationship that just wasn't meant to be, because we're both even-tempered "happy" people, and talking about any of that causes the friendship we're both (over)planning to have to not work. I'll be glad to see you the next time that happens, and I won't have the right to even care about how you behave in relation to any situation with Rob from now on, and it's a weight off my shoulders to know that you're my friend, and that with you in my "friendship file", I don't get to worry about what you're doing or how you're acting towards me or towards anyone else. And that's enough talking about a friendship that should just happen, not be planned out…haha. See ya soon, I'm guessing. Til then…

-Bruce

(ps-despite what I just said, I reserve the right to punch you in the face if I ever hear you call another guy Scrump ;)

So it would seem as though we were both on the same page about breaking up, going our separate ways, and just being friends… right? Well, apparently something happened that led to "psychotic text messages." Anyway, here's the next email I sent him just two and a half hours later:

At 9:08pm, the same day (8/24/2010):

I think maybe seeing me happy is what's got you sending all these psychotic text messages, who knows. Know this though: I broke up with you with absolutely no 'other guy' in mind. I don't wanna be with you because you're not a good boyfriend, not in the ways I need someone to be. I gave Kristine a detailed description of each reason I know you aren't someone I need to be dating that night, before any party or I had fun (again, I know my happiness angers you, and I apologize?). I will try to keep you from any knowledge that my life is going well if it really upsets you that much, but I see that you're going to continue to try and make this more difficult than it needs to be. I have NEVER dated any1 who spoke with or saw an ex EVER once we started dating. Asking me once more what to do in response to Rob and letting me know you were thinking the 'no response to his text msg', even though he's ALWAYS showed up when u've done that in the past, showsme that you're retarded. Keeley, another rational person, told me tonight on the phone that Rob says you like it when he brings Tinker over. Well the 3 of u can spend as much or as little time together as you like from now on because your behavior makes me want nothing to do with you. Fuck friendship, because even though you say that's what you want, YOU DON'T. Recognize the pattern: I dump you with no intention of getting back together because you wont change, then you flip out over some behavior of mine AFTER WE ARE BROKEN UP (so u have no right to be mad about it), and then I get manipulated into being with you somehow through ur texting craziness. Well I don't wanna be with you! If it helps you to think it's all me, then that's fine. But please stop texting me, slandering my character and thinking every time u've ever hurt my feelings was made up. Being physically abusive would have been better than this shit. I'm done. The pedestal u put yourself on, and the gutter you throw me down into doesn't make me think I'm lucky to be with you. I'm an idiot for thinking I could teach you to understand how to be a good boyfriend. Ask Kristine if you really wanna change for the better, but I know you don't. U just wanna keep thinking how u always have, that any1 who sees your flaws is the crazy 1. Bye

I do not know what happened from here, but my fear is the exact pattern of behavior I outlined in the email is what he did, and we stayed together. Which makes me the r*tarded one, really. (I know we don't use that word anymore!!)

> **We were built to fall apart**
> **And fall back together.**
> **-Out of the Woods**, Taylor Swift

On September 18th he was buying us tickets to go see Lady Gaga, so somehow, we got through that. She was awesome!! "You & I" hadn't been released yet, but she played it with her bright-yellow hair. She is a rock star.

CHAPTER 19

Pot, meet Kettle.

I was friends with a guy in his mid-thirties who was in law enforcement at the time when we met. Oddly enough, he told me one night at the club, "Hey, if you ever get a ticket out in Carolina Beach, let me know and I'll see what I can do to help get you out of it." I have no doubt he said this thinking it would never happen, just being nice. Well, whether it was that night or the following night, I cannot recall; all I know is those words were fresh on my mind when I found myself getting pulled over, in the car with Keeley, having just dropped a mutual friend off at her mom's Carolina Beach condo. The officer asked me, "Sir, do you know how fast you were going over that bridge!?" When the officer walked back to his patrol car, I asked my friend, "What bridge?" She and I had a tendency to get wrapped up too deeply in conversation to notice much of anything…

Luckily for me, I had a very new friend in law enforcement to save the day. He helped me out of my ticket and named me an honorary lifeguard! And nothing "weird" or "inappropriate" occurred between us; it was just a nice thing he did for me.

So imagine my confusion when Jon and Jean were out by the pool with me, giving me hell for calling this man my friend. Based on rumors and gossip, Jean and Jon insisted I "open my eyes" and see that he was a "creep." They were essentially bullying me for being "naive" because I didn't like making sweeping judgment calls based on rumors, especially given that all of the rumors I'd heard about this man came from Jon and Jean. Based on my firsthand experiences, he was a super nice guy and a good friend to have. And to this day that is what I think of him, based on my own experiences.

What's so interesting is the things that they were trying to tell me were so bad about this guy were vague at best, like that he'd "done something inappropriate" with one of the lifeguards working under him.

Sidenote: Having a boyfriend who tries to make you feel foolish is not a good feeling. Two fortyfivish-year-old bullies were my chosen company for the day, apparently. Today, this would also be a major red flag for me…but at the time I just needed answers. And as someone who doesn't like talking behind someone's back, I went straight to the source. I asked Officer Smithers if we could talk. So we went to Waffle House and had a chat. I asked him every question I could think of regarding the rumors I'd been fed by the pool that day. He explained that the lifeguard I'd heard about was a gay young man who was kicked out of his home by his homophobic parents and needed a place to stay. When the parents found out where he was staying, they decided it was "inappropriate." And maybe it was inappropriate. But so is making your kid homeless.

And so is making fun of your boyfriend for believing there are good people in the world.

CHAPTER 20

Money in the Bag

Prior to dating Jon, I had very limited gambling knowledge. I knew Jon often played poker locally with a group of guys at various locations. And I knew that a lot of the guys that would come over to the house were "poker people." Jon was getting more and more involved with online casinos, which allowed him to improve his poker game while also playing for real money any time he wanted to 24-7. He was big into this before he and I started dating.

I just flashed back to a memory of Rob fussing at a hand he was certain he had won in online poker while playing in Jon's office. I was not into it but certainly willing to be around it and support my friends. All couples should have both overlapping as well as their own individual interests, right? I sooo wish I'd avoided this one. But it was such a big part of Jon's world at this time. And apparently I'd decided I wanted to be a part of that world (cue *Little Mermaid* music).

Jon explained his reason for dating young guys is simply that he likes the way their faces light up when experiencing things for the first time. In June 2010, Jon took us out to Vegas. I'd say this was one of those "first time experiences" he had talked about; it was all new to me. I was wowed! Not to mention the amazing hotel rooms that are comped for high rollers and the extra special treatment Jon got for being one of those elites. The flashing lights of the casinos…and there being so many different casinos; it was all exciting. So when we weren't having sex in the hotel room with the HUGE windows and bathroom the casino was the obvious place to be. And just because

I didn't play poker didn't mean I couldn't hang, and slots I could handle. And Jon was enjoying showing me around. I'd sit with him at a table or we'd sit next to each other at a couple of slot machines. He was funding this, so don't get it twisted. Given that my paychecks still came from his hotel at this point I was not expected to be dropping those paychecks into these machines. Plus, he tended to like high roller slots and wasn't going to waste his time with the ones I would've gone for if I were on my own dime anyway. Although I've heard penny slots can result in killer cash payouts… (*That last line was a terrible joke that only one person may find amusing.)

*Suggested Listen: **Getaway Car** -Taylor Swift

We came back from Vegas, and I knew a little more about poker and gambling now. So rather than just ask Jon as I walked through the office, "How's it going, are you winning?" I knew the basics of how to play. And I was curious…so…

October 18, 2010, is when I signed up for Full Tilt Poker. ((This was a big mistake.))

It was a big mistake because over the time I was with Jon, I managed to lose a considerable amount of money to this ridiculousness. And by "a considerable amount", I'm glad I don't know the dollar amount. It would definitely be a six-figure number though. It includes an investment account my parents set up for me when I was a kid. So yeah, a lot of money that could've been saved or better spent. But hey, we needed a shared hobby! Right? (Sooo stupid.) Although we did spend a lot of time together playing. Still, the juice was not worth the squeeze.

This is one addiction I gained while in this relationship that I've been able to get away from in the present day. So…hey…it could be worse, I guess? Oh yeah, and smoking cigarettes — Jon and I were both nonsmokers at this point, come to think of it, and had been for a while.

Now, before I make it sound like gambling was all terrible all the time, it was not. We also took a trip to the Hard Rock Casino in Florida. Jon and I entered a poker tournament — the first I'd ever played, live — and I won. By "won", I mean it got down to ten people and we chopped the pot. I walked away with $3,500, which was cool. Had I never played online, I absolutely would not have had any success in this tournament because I wouldn't have known how to play well enough to pull this off.

CHAPTER 21

We Were Happy

Jon and I had a lot of fun together. I had a lot of fun with Jon. Admittedly, we had way too much sex. At least once a day, marathon-style sex. We did it at my apartment, on the couch, the bed, the ottoman, and the portable cheetah sling Jon brought with him. At his home, on the bed, in a leather-and-chain sling, in the upstairs bedroom we turned into a sex room, or in the attic when the sex room was in the attic. In the pool house, by the pool, on the roof of the night club (a few times), in his office in his desk chair. He was a big fan of mirrors and cameras. In the shower/steam room. At his hotel, in any of the rooms we stayed in (when we were on the run from Rob). And fortunately, Jon was pretty great in bed. When we would have sex, afterward he would always say, "You're trying to kill me!" and we would laugh. I would frequently tell him to "touch my tongue" because it was dry like sandpaper because I was so dehydrated. Had Jon not been sexually charged like me, that first year and a half probably would have been boring. I'm not sure we had much in common, given that I didn't pick up my poker obsession until nine months in...

At some point he gave me the go-ahead to get a saltwater aquarium. I can't remember which one was first, the one in the pool house or the house. Wait, yes, I do, it was the house, house. I know this because I asked Jon one day, dead serious, "What direction do you see the tank going...?" as if he was going to know what the fuck that meant. There are fish only, fish only with live rock, SPS tanks, soft coral tanks, seahorse tanks, and on and on and on. Jon didn't know any of that. He said it back to me, like, "I don't know Brucifer, what direction do *you* think the tank should go?" We laughed. But that kept me entertained, along with enrolling in grad school and working constantly.

November 8th, 2010 is when I got my "Welcome" email for grad school. Early in our relationship I was hired to work at the local mental hospital. I went through the interview process…I got hired, officially! I then waited for the HR department to call with my start date…and waited…and waited. Then I called them, only to be told that myself and three others who had been hired for the Psych Tech position would not actually be starting because the hospital's funding had been cut. This was very disheartening to say the least. This town did not have a lot of behavioral health options at that time, and without further schooling, my psychology degree from the local university was only going to get me so far.

An event we traveled to that I personally enjoyed very much was Creamfields in November 2010. With thirty thousand attendees at the electronic music festival in Buenos Aires, I was overwhelmed in the best of ways. I've always loved music and crowds, concerts, dance parties, nightclubs, and this was all of those things times ten. From where I was standing, it was *amazing*! (Check it out on YouTube if you need a visual). David Guetta was there performing, and it was during the time he was blowing up. It was such a great show and a truly once-in-a-lifetime experience.

Creamfields was very much "our" vibe (I know my vibe, and he picked and booked the trip, so "our" vibe it is). Great music, thirty thousand people, *fun*!

Jon and I are both upbeat and friendly people. You would think we could get along no matter what. And for the most part, we had a lot of fun. When we'd find ourselves off track, we'd get through these times relatively easily, I'd say. Then we'd just have sex. We really didn't have any issues when we were having sex. It was always when communication, or life, or needs, or any of those other things came up that there was a problem.

Creamfields was one of the first times I realized **fighting with him was like trying to solve a crossword and realizing there's no right answer.**

We were in the middle of a *huge* crowd where we had been dancing, sweating, and having a great time. And it was certainly hot. Suddenly my mouth went completely dry as it does sometimes. I think we were on acid. (I know we were on acid later that day, but I'm pretty sure we were on it at this time.) And so I kind of panicked because I was going to have to get out of this crowd to get to water and it had suddenly become urgent. When my mouth does this, it redefines the phrase "dry swallow"; it is bad. So I beelined it. I am not an anxious person but this was not the time to have a desert mouth. Jon followed behind me. I was moving as quickly (but politely) as I could through the crowd. When I finally got out of it and to a water hut or whatever, Jon was flustered, questioning, "Why'd you just storm away like that!?" As I was desperately gulping down water, I thought that one was obvious, but I explained that my mouth had done the "touch my tongue" thing and I couldn't swallow (thinking "touch my tongue" would click for him). He dug in over the idea that I had meant it to be something dramatic about him, but it simply was not. I didn't want to get away from him, I wanted to get water! I thought surely with the "touch my tongue" reference he'd get it. I still can't imagine why escaping the one person I know out of thirty thousand makes more sense than my explanation that I was dehydrated. You know what would've been really great to hear in this moment? "I care about you." "I was worried about you." "When you started chugging that water I realized you looked distressed. Are you okay?" or maybe even, "I thought about what you might be experiencing and not just about how it was impacting me…" Well, that last one I didn't so much want to hear that as I would've loved if he'd ever adopted that attitude.

But anyway…

The idea that dating younger guys is preferable because of the excitement on their faces as they experience new things for the first time is a lovely sentiment. Certainly Creamfields was such an experience, absolutely.

Creamfields was amazing. This dehydrated moment certainly didn't ruin the festivities.

But if I insisted that my tongue felt like sandpaper and that rushing away was simply beelining it to get water because I was dehydrated, and my boyfriend then doesn't believe me...where do you even go from there?

I think of it like the **All Too Well** (Taylor Swift) short film. Did he drop her hand? *Obviously!* But I try to see things from all angles; maybe both perspectives can have merit? If all-too-well Jake *really* doesn't remember...or if Jon *felt like* I'd "stormed off," who's to say? But in that moment, it temporarily derailed the mood. Both mine and Taylor's. LOL.

Jon tended to get flustered very quickly then he was over it like it never happened, which in little instances like this was great. I just wanted water, not an argument, not to be distrusted, and not to get away from Jon. So when he dropped it I was good to do the same.

Leaving in the taxi from the show literally as Fatboy Slim took the stage as we pulled away was also disheartening, but ultimately fine. It was an amazing event and I had a blast.

So back to the fact that we were tripping on acid. Well, when you're in Buenos Aires in a taxi, they play a game that feels similar to bumper cars...driving aggressively in a tight space...going really fast! The only difference is...no one bumps into each other. But when you're an American in the back seat freaking out, let me assure you, if you have someone back there with you, insisting, "No, he's really not driving like a lunatic, and we're going to be *fine*," it's in that moment you'll be really glad that Jon is there. And when he doesn't miss a beat and says, "Have I ever told you, you have a hairy tongue?" It's in that moment you laugh and the acid paranoia subsides. **#LuckyOnes**

CHAPTER 22

Mental Gymnastics and Mind Fucks

The Axel Hotel is a luxury hotel specifically for gay clientele. Jon and I stayed here when we were in Buenos Aires. This hotel has a rooftop pool with a glass bottom, so from the hotel's lobby, you can see guests swimming in the pool from underneath. Certainly a unique feature, as well as a cool thing to observe as you're checking in. Dudes in Speedos, observed from underneath— clever marketing. And I'm sure it attracts a lot of business. I believe it was a major factor in Jon picking this hotel.

I knew from being friends with Rob and Jon that they fooled around with other guys, typically together, I think, or at least that was my perception, going into a relationship with Jon. I didn't know the details of what they did. I just brought my own experience with me into this relationship with Jon, which had been monogamy-only. And I guess I wouldn't say I was opposed to other ways of being in a relationship…wait, that's not true. If I'm being real right now, I hadn't really taken the time to consider being nonmonogamous in any form or fashion. So not that I was opposed to it, I just was of the mindset to expect monogamy, making anything different a new consideration…and not one I got much time to consider either. There was never a discussion with Jon about this change in our relationship, it was more like in the moment I'm expected to know the game has changed and be on board with the new rules.

Here's how that played out: There was a dude in a tan Speedo. Jon asked me if I found him attractive. Not particularly. Nice body, but I wasn't wild about his face. I thought we were just people-watching at this point. Not to mention I'm sure I was a bit jealous because again, my backstory had been monogamy-based.

The next day, Jon was gone when I woke up. He came back to the room, explaining he'd gone for a swim. As we're walking out of the hotel in search of a bite to eat (I think?), someone from the front desk— maybe a manager— started speaking across the lobby at Jon and me, explaining, "So sorry sir, we didn't mean to be rude. I truly hope it did not come across that way, it's just that we cannot have guests swimming in the pool without clothes on…we do hope you understand, and there are signs explaining that all the guests must be in swimwear when using the pool." (The man looked up.) "I'm sure you can understand why we have this rule…" The whole time this man was speaking Jon was attempting to cut him off, but this man was insistent on getting through his entire speech.

I was a little confused, not because I gave a shit that he was swimming naked, but if he'd been yelled at by the staff of the hotel, why didn't he come back to the room and tell me about it? It was something we could've laughed about, had he bothered to mention it. (If tan Speedo guy was around for naked swim time, I'll never know…it would make more sense as to why Jon hadn't mentioned this event, but this is just me speculating.)

That evening I was voluntold I would be hanging out with Tan Speedo's Asian friend while Jon and Tan Speedo hung out, separately. Um…ok… Luckily, the Asian friend was super hot. Jon and I hadn't played around with other people separately from each other before. I figured that by going along with this, I was being the chill boyfriend that apparently I was expected to be. However, when I got back to the room and Jon asked what we had gotten into and I told Jon we'd had (protected) sex, Jon informed me that he and Tan Speedo had hooked up but not gone all the way. This is probably not what Taylor was referring to when she sang **never impressed by me acing your tests**, but I'd imagine the feeling is similar. So I didn't even get to be happy that Mr. Asian friend was dynamite in bed; instead, **all I felt was shame**...

If there had been a conversation about potentially hooking up with other people ahead of time...well, who knows? But there wasn't. Jon sort of just let me know he'd be hanging out with "rando" in the tan bathing suit, and I was to go with the "other rando." Now that I'm thinking about it, I'm wondering if those guys were both escorts...? But there wasn't even enough conversation about the matter before it was happening for me to glean that information. The following became a pattern: If others were coming to bed with us, Jon knew first, and I'd find out. *But when?* Always on a delay that was totally avoidable WITH COMMUNICATION. There would be someone walking behind us on the way back to the house from the club, and *then* Jon would bother to clue me in, having already spoken to the third party at some point...whether it was a friend/acquaintance...or a porn "actor"/go-go dancer. And it always felt like the third party knew more about what was about to happen than I did. *This* was the worst feeling. Knowing a paid from-out-of-town go-go boy had more knowledge of what we'd be getting into back at the house than I did, and not because I lack spontaneity, but because my own boyfriend hadn't mentioned he'd invited company who had sexual expectations. You really and truly cannot put a price on what it feels like to have full consent. I'm thinking now that maybe there's a world in which a boyfriend is appreciative of getting an escort paid for by their boyfriend, but that was not me. At least not without a prior conversation in which I was given all of the facts. And where I had *some* say in who the dude was.

Before I go sounding like a complete prude, there were other times when Jon approached it like, "Hey, Brucey, anyone here (at the bar) that you think *we* would wanna take home tonight?" And *that* I was totally on board with once I'd left behind the idea that monogamy was best. Because in these instances, I had a say in the matter. Or when we'd fuck around with friends or afterparties devolved into sex parties...that was all golden. It was when I was put on the spot because a third person had been told either we...or sometimes just I...would be hooking up with them later before I had been given this information; that's when it became more of a disconnect between Jon and me, and that's when it didn't sit well. Only one of these times was I emphatically like, "I don't care what you've told that person, I will not be hooking up with him." And to that person, I am sorry because it WAS NOT about you. It was about Jon's tendency to tell me who I'd be sleeping with instead of asking me if I wanted to sleep with someone. And *yes*, there is a *huge* difference between these two things.

In my work as a therapist, I have found that for couples attempting to make an open relationship of any kind work and keep it healthy, there has to be really strong communication. At the time of the above story, I did not want to be in an open relationship. And we never really were in an open relationship; we were just in a relationship where Jon **changed the rules every day**. I knew I wasn't allowed to just go off and sleep with people when we were in our home city, but I came to learn that if we were leaving the bar and Jon said someone was coming home with us, the expectation was that I should be down for whatever. And if I wanted to bring someone home with us, Jon inevitably obliged, and then just spoke ill of the person in whispers and then at normal volume once they were gone…even though they were young, attractive, and under any other circumstance they would have been totally his type. But whatever. Now that it's been typed I can set it free!

CHAPTER 23

Better than Revenge

*Suggested listen: **Better Than Revenge**, Taylor Swift

This song just came on shuffle and this is pretty much the best place for this side story! Thanks for looking out, Taylor! In this chapter, it's actually going to be Rob singing Taylor's part…

Two random things happened in the early days of my relationship with Jon, both of which were baffling and neither of which were accurately attributed to the mastermind, until years later…

The first is that I got a call from the Health Department explaining I'd been exposed to syphilis. Yikes! That shit will rot your brain! I had no symptoms and was pretty sexually responsible, believe it or not. And I knew I wasn't going to be a walking disease (LOL)! So I went to get checked at the Health Department, although Jon and I were out of town, so it wasn't the local one. Not to mention, I had to tell Jon about the call and why we had to go, which was embarrassing. But I also knew I hadn't cheated on him, so it was whatever. I don't know if this is how they do it everywhere, but they take your blood for the test, then treat you with the tremendous ass shot of penicillin, *then* they tell you your test results. So I got pumped full of antibiotics I did not need, and it was painful. And while I was glad to know the test was negative, I could not think for the life of me how I had been exposed…?

Thanks for making that false report to the Health Department, Rob 😊! Note: This has never been confirmed to have been him, I just know that it was. This next event is the reason I can say it was him with relative confidence...

Rob also got me fired from a job. Apparently, he called the mental health hospital I worked at in Jacksonville and told them something that led them to ask me to go to LabCorp for a drug test. I knew something about this was weird; they didn't do random drug testing. During orientation, the instructor had even made a point to tell us about this guy who worked at the hospital who had showed up smelling like weed every day, but they couldn't fire him or send him for drug testing because their policies wouldn't allow it! So instead of driving to LabCorp I drove home and found that page in my orientation binder to be sure I wasn't crazy and brought it back to them. They said they were sending me for the drug test because of an "anonymous call."

Speaking to Jon about this, he convinced me it was the front desk manager at his hotel that had called. At least that was his best guess. I mean, this guy was a prick but not particularly out to get me, but I couldn't think of anyone else, so I assumed Jon was right. It wasn't until a couple of years later that Kris McRay casually mentioned, "Oh, you know, that was Rob who did that...right?"

That made a lot more sense. And in the chance that Rob ever reads these words, just know that I ain't mad atcha. I actually think it's pretty funny.

CHAPTER 24

Back to December

Kris came back into the picture. It was a mess. It was not a sexual affair; it was worse. It was totally emotional. But given the intensity of our emotions and those damn butterflies that just would not stay dead, it caused a lot of problems.

Not to shirk responsibility or point the finger of blame, but riddle me this: Who would move their boyfriend's ex-boyfriend onto the property, especially when he had so much up close and personal knowledge of the emotional intensity there had been? Well, Jon would! Apparently, that's who!

I'm not blaming Jon for my feelings for Kris being reignited; he was doing a nice thing (and it also made his work helper immediately accessible, which was no doubt a plus). And maybe it was bound to happen, it just definitely happened sooner and more easily due to proximity...

It's killing me to see you go after all this time. -Breathe, Taylor Swift

Email from Jon (January 24, 2011):

Bruce,

Without trying to point out the things that brought us to where we are I want to let you

> know that I have had a great time being with you. As much as I know what we are doing is the right thing extracting you from my heart is not an easy thing to do. My stoic demeanor hides my sadness and I think it is important that you know that no matter what you see on the outside the reality of not having you in my life in the same way weighs heavy on my heart. I will always remember you by the happy memories.
>
> This note is not intended to initiate reconciliation. I write it because my feelings are not always clear and I don't want you to leave here thinking that I have a cold heart. I hope we are able to maintain a lifelong friendship and I wish you and Kris or whoever you end up with the happiest and most fulfilling of times during your entire stay on this here planet or any other for that matter.
>
> xo

Jon did not say emotional things often. So when he wrote emails like the one above, they were pretty effective. I know that the words say "goodbye" and don't imply any chance at reconciliation, but the underlying, louder message— at least to me— was don't leave. Maybe I'm just reading it how I want it to read, but again, when Jon brought just about any admission that he was having a feeling into the equation, it definitely impacted how I responded behaviorally.

I wrote back to Jon the same day (1/24/2011):

> You are a goof ball. and you're stuck with me til I have somewhere else to live, so other than sexy time, nothing is really all that different. I am gonna start looking into finding somewhere to move tho, so don't worry, I won't be in your (less grey) hair much longer :)

Sorry if this response lacks the sentiment that your message had. and again, you are a goof ball.

I hope you'll take what I said to heart, especially the 1st and last part... ;)

Remember what I said earlier about relationships that break up and get back together being the unhealthy ones?...

During our emotional entanglement, I remember I sent Kris the written-out lyrics to "**Back to December**" (by Taylor Swift)... but I had made one minor alteration...

**I miss your ~~tan~~ pale skin, your sweet smile
So good to me, so right**

In the email above, Jon was not wrong. I was definitely leaning toward calling it quits for real, walking away, and trying to do so on peaceful terms.

Email from Jon about sixteen days after our last exchange (2/10/2011) titled "We Are Not Meant to be Together":

when i run everything through that has brought us to where we are and try to take a impartial observers view (not entirely possible i know) here is what i see... but first let me lay down the not so impartial observers observations.

Bruce and Jon seem to be in a committed relationship and seem happy with each other for the most part Jon is quite a bit older than bruce but young in spirit and has aged well. Bruces youthful 25 years and looks younger. bruce is a bright bubbly fellow who lights up a room when he walks into it and keeps a positive outlook on life. and he love to disrupt the fish and coral in his two salt water fish tanks every chance he gets. he is mildly embarrassed by his aquariumophilia and sometimes feels the need to hide the true extent of his enthusiasm for the tanks or the hours devoted to them. he graduated from college a little over 2 years ago and has had a couple of jobs in mental health as a stepping stone to grad school. after the most recent job ended about 6 months ago has been unsuccessful to date finding another job and is now looking into graduate schools. bruce's positive aura, friendly approachable personality, combined with his confidence and smashing looks make him a joy to be around an instant friend to almost everyone he comes in contact.

Jon is a good hearted spirit who like to approach everything he does with a combination of passion energy and urgency. unemployed for the past 10 years he has gradually settled into the role of project manager for his real estate and business holdings. he spends alot of time doing renovation work with a small crew of helpers and tends to grab onto the efforts like a dog to a bone until complete. he is easy to get along with and will talk with anyone about anything. and talk he will. friends tend expect his long rambling commentaries and depending on the topic are tolerant, amused (with rolling eyes) or they will cut him off. he is often portrayed as unapproachable and while he does not go out of his way to change this perception anyone that knows him would disagree. dont be fooled by his sometimes dimwitted and forgetful persona the words sometime have trouble leaving the mouth but he observes, understands, and is sensitive to what is going on in his world. he is easy going yet caring attributes that contribute to him being a genuinely good guy. these attributes also make him an easy target for those who want to take advantage of one of his other attributes generosity.

giving an opinion is made difficult by both Jon and bruces addiction to meth which they seem to everyday all day long/. it is hard to say if the drug helps hold them together tears them apart or is not a factor. another common obstacle to rendering an accurate opinion is they both at time seem to be easy to dismiss the relationship however they both try to explain their reasoning later in the report.

i was asked to begin my study of these two lovable fellows around the end of december but i decided to dig a little deeper and get some additional background. here are some of the things i have learned in order of occurrence.

- bruce and Jon came to know each other about 5 years ago through Jons then boyfriend. the boyfriend and bruce were good friends and as it turned out the boyfriend had a worsening bipolar or personality disorder that made him difficult to manage. Jon attempted to end the relationship many times with varying degrees of success. out of frustration Jon turned to bruce to help him keep rob in check or distracted during the many attempts to Jon tried to extract himself from this difficult sick man. in late august 2009 Jon and bruces relationship began to shift and by late november they were in a full blown relationship.
- the ex boyfriend continued to cling on to the hope that he would get back with Jon and in late december bruce express his feelings

that Jon was not being forceful enough in his desire rob to leave me alone. Jon said he understood and that despite his best effort short of something drastic he was also at the end of his rope. both bruce and Jon up until this time were working together and were trying to unveil our relationship with the least pain delivered to the ex especially in light of the fact that bruce and rob had been best friends.

- it wasnt until january that this issue started to begin to resolve itself however there are lingering jolts of the ex into their life to this day. around this time premised on the issue of rob bruce had taken an opportunity to deceptively rendezvous with a customer staying in the hotel where bruce worked. Jon found out about it and bruce initially insisted there was nothing deceptive of inappropriate about what he did because he broke up in the care on the way to the bar to meet them. the reason for the break up was no longer wanting to have to deal with rob although until then it was a partnership between bruce and Jon to extract ourselves from his badgering.
- the relationship quickly got back on track and it was for the most part smooth sailing until august when rob again poked his self into their lives one to many times and bruce decided to end it/ according to Jon bruce seemed unusually euphoric to be out of the relationship and among other things had a couple of parties at Jons house the first one held on the day they broke up sending Jon the signal that the relationship meant nothing. this was in spite of what from the out-

side appeared to be a healthy happy relationship other than the rob factor.
- the recovery from that was quick despite Jons discloser of a whole series of emails left up on a computer indicating he had not been entirely faithful. Jon said that he loved bruce enough to put the behavior behind like he did in january for the sake of saving the relationship
- again smooth sailing until november both came away with a unspoken belief that the other was more interested in finding other people than being with the other. this was not revealed by either until recently. during his hiatus from work bruce has picked up Jon's passion for on line poker and is learning the game well. it seemed like in the beginning of the relationship Jon's attention to poker was partly coming at bruce's expense but recognizing this Jon cut back… this role seemed to flipflop when bruce picked up the poker bug with a vengeance and focus. meaningful conversation was difficult for a period when bruce was playing cards and he was playing 18 hours a day
- the relationship began to improve from there but bruce was getting isolated from the lack of work and the antisocial effects of the meth. they both were more and are more reclusive in part due to the meth. Jons friend Kris mcray was also bruces x boyfriend but Kris and i had talked alot about bruce over the time bruce and i were together and was adamant in his not having any desire or want to go back to a relationship with bruce likewise bruce had been over the top in his attacks on

Kris some that were not fair/ bruce was very angry he had wasted the time with Kris that he had. Kris was relieved not to have bruces constant attempts to remold him into what bruce wanted him to be. Jon tryed to foster a friendship between them because despite their not wanting to be in a relationship he felt like they should be friends.

- Kris was homeless and without a car or money and as a friend Jon felt some need to help kris and asked bruce if it was ok if kris spent a few nights in the pool house while a made a few dollars working for Jon. by the end of december Jon became concerned over the way bruce and kris were interacting. Jon at first was glad that bruce was coming out of his shell but quickly saw things going in the wrong direction, Jon still felt like it would pass and that bruce seemed so happy to have another person besides Jon to hang out with and to help relieve bruces isolation. Jon made bruce aware of his concerns in early january and was accused of just not wanting bruce to have any friends and that nothing was happening. according to Jon bruces behavior only became more blatant. Jon felt like the flaunting of the affair was insensitive, intentional and especially cruel. in light of the fact that Jon had ask for it to end. Jon in frustration made the comment to Kris mcray that he could fuck my boyfriend. the comment was not the right way to handle it and Jon apologized and explained what drove him there. but as with any of the other times on the subject did bruce give Jon any sense of comfort he only made statements that were at best evasive

- after the incident with the texting and going back with Kris to the hotel for so long Jon felt like bruce was spelling it out clear as day so Jon decided to do bruce the favor of an easy out.
- unfortunately as angry and as disrespected insensitive as Jon felt he had been done he realized that we had had a good relationship prior to Kris and that if he let bruce go and he got back with Kris he would not be any happier than with me and he felt like kris was a relief valve to bruces isolation
- Jon lays out his feelings and gets what he believes is bruces desire to rebuild our relationship and that he was not in a relationship with Kris.
- bruce so far has to Jon's knowledge not broken off relations with Kris but instead has answered my questions posed by Jon about the two of them with messages that say basically if you were only Kris mcrey and and that his head is fucked up words that give Jon doubts not reassurance. again statements that are at best avoiding the answer and at worst stating u want to be with Kris. sometime i think i could be with him are counterproductive if the intention is to be with someone else. if i told you some of the things he said to me that made me feel so special you would think i was mean" i would agree but isn't the statement alone mean and insensitive particularly when the request was regarding you and me and every response was about Kris <8:24 AM>

To me that doesn't read as "We are not meant to be together." It reads as "I have concerns you're still into your ex-boyfriend and am looking for reassurance that's not the case." It's just a really long-winded way of making that point.

Later that same day, Jon wrote:

> sorry to be such a wus and emailing you instead of just saying whats on my mind but i get too wound up and unable to properly articulate my thoughts. anyway here it is
>
> it just hit me like a ton of bricks. i think at the core of it all is i just dont feel any passion from you and thats why i seem so willing to give u up. i mean tonight i feel like i was spurned at every attempt i made at intimacy i feel uncomfortable sitting in there while you jerk off unsure of what u want. none of my stabs at reconciliation were met with any enthusiasm this evening so if there is any desire to to stay together you you hide it very well. the lack of passion is something you cannot change on demand without it being fake. Either you have it or you dont. there may be the slight possibility that you feel it but cant express it and if thats the case let me know

*Suggested listen: **All You Had to Do Was Stay** -Taylor Swift

Six months with no passion, no employment, where I'm not in school and isolated? I don't even remember this time period; it's like it has been edited out of my mind. I mean, we did a lot of GHB, and that can cause memory loss. But this sounds different...

The idea that I had a "party" in the pool house to "celebrate a break up" is exaggerated and false. There was no theme we were celebrating and it was mostly his friends...like, six people, total. I got scolded for having those people over. Then when I get close to

Kris, I'm then told I need to cut him off (now, granted, the Kris part is much more understandable). Jon says he doesn't want me isolated, but when I invite people to the pool house to hang out, I end up in the dog house. None of these people had any idea Jon and I were on the rocks, which makes it a bit ridiculous that he'd decided the party was themed about us breaking up. But the take-home message I get is actually that Jon is hurting and that I'm not helping to ease that hurt. And I get that.

*Suggested listen: **Anti-Hero** – Taylor Swift

At the time of this email exchange, we'd agreed that I would move out into the pool house while looking for somewhere to live since I'd sublet my apartment. We had always slept in the same bed, so moving to the pool house (even if only briefly) was…something. Clearly breaking up made the most sense. He didn't just kick me off the property, he's not a complete asshole.

I don't think it was that evening; it must've been the next. He went out to dinner with some of our mutual friends. Jon extended an invite to me to join if I wanted, but I declined because it was too soon and too weird since we weren't a couple anymore and he was going to dinner with friends that were a couple. While he was out at dinner, I came into the house because the pool house TV didn't have functional cable at the time. Whenever he arrived back, he came into the house where I was watching tv and said "Oh…this is awkward…"

What was?

He'd brought back two guys— both younger than me, both of whom I knew (one of whom I'd fucked, the other I would fuck many years later, but that's irrelevant). They'd come back to the house to "go for a swim." Neither of these were people he'd told me he was going to dinner with, so how he managed this I have no idea.

I don't know if this was a ploy to make me jealous or if he was just (what felt like) "auditioning" new boyfriends before I was even off the property…or if he'd just somehow run into two cute young gay dudes that begged him to let them come for a swim. Who the fuck knows?

Rather than overthink what was going on, we all just went for a swim. Jon offered everyone some GHB. The dose I took— poured by Jon, handed to me by Jon— knocked me out, so I have no recollection of what the other three did that evening. (For anyone who doesn't know this, there is an amount of GHB you can take to remain conscious and be high, which is the goal, and remember everything from the evening. Two drops more, and you're likely to remain conscious but act like a complete idiot and have little to no ability to reel it in, but you remember the experience the next day. Two drops more, and someone is telling you the next day how you behaved because you have no recollection but remained awake. Two drops more, and you pass out just about the minute it hits you, unconscious, and you're asleep/down for the count.)

Being drugged into slumberville should have resulted in continued momentum toward breaking up and getting the hell out of there, right? It did not. Both of those guys were gone when I came to, and since we were technically broken up at the time this happened, I didn't think of it as Jon cheating. ((Random: They're both pretty good in bed, so I'm not sure if the "audition" wasn't all it was cracked up to be or what.))

What followed may've been the one memorable pseudo-apology I got over the six-year relationship. If I'm not mistaken, he bought flowers and I even got a handwritten note on the flower tag, which I held onto for a long time and may even still have somewhere. *(You know how some people have a shoe box with mementos from a relationship? This card would literally be the one thing I have from this man that would fit into that category. It's about the size of a business card; it's only a sentence, maybe two. But it was sweet.)* To be clear, I am typically someone who apologizes easily when I have wronged someone and I have no problem admitting if I misspoke or gave bad info or whatever. But when your partner does not share that way of being, you stop admitting when you're wrong too, as it will only be used against you.

> **My mistake, I didn't know to be in love**
> **You had to fight to have the upper hand.**
>   -**White Horse**, Taylor Swift

Somehow we did not break up and I did not move off property at this time, despite what I said in that second email.

I'll never know if Jon's "apology" was driven by guilt or by love and sincerity. (I'm putting "apology" in quotes, because the card said something about realizing what he stood to lose, which he realized when I was sleeping. It didn't say "I'm sorry" – but that was the sentiment behind the gesture, I think. Although…) I think it's entirely possible he was afraid I'd tell people. Dudes who overdose others on G are not typically "good" dudes…I may never know his motives, truly. And **the more I think about it now, the less I know…** Consequence avoidance versus genuine remorse? Who's to say?. I can't speak for him. Again, it *feels* more likely, I'm not stating it as a fact. And since I'm not making any statements of fact in this paragraph, I'll go ahead and say the aforementioned card said something like "watching you sleep I got to imagine you were mine for a minute." It felt like a sweet card when I read it. Better than nothing? Worth salvaging a relationship over? My mind and heart were very disconnected, let's just say.

Jon was **wild and crazy. Just so frustrating. Intoxicating. Complicated…** now it sounds like the passion is gone…at least from Jon's perspective.

> **Never knew I could feel that much**
> **And that's the way I loved you.**
> **-The Way I Loved You**, Taylor Swift

In the last email, Jon mentioned that I'd been playing 18 hours of poker a day, and that was on February 10, 2011. Then on February 15th, 2011 I posted on Facebook that I "got to go deep sea fishing yesterday, then won >$3k in a poker tournament last night." Sounds like practice makes perfect!

March 1st 2011, I started my job at Shell Island Resort on Wrightsville Beach.

May 16th, 2011, according to Facebook, I was laying out by the pool with the double threat! Blackie and Brownie were the newest editions to our world and the cutest little dogs I ever did see! They were born in March and now they are here!

In August of 2011, we went and spent time with his family in Maine. His family members are awesome.

September we went to the Outer Banks and had a great time hanging out at the beach. There were ten of us total and we had a really fun time out at Kill Devil Hills.

September 19th, 2011 is when we made it "Facebook official" that we were dating. (We'd been together for, like, almost two years at this point, but there was never a rush to make things public.)

On September 29th, I was in Atlanta for my first academic residency for grad school, on my way toward becoming what was, at the time, a Licensed Professional Counselor.

On December 1st, 2011, I started a new job at the Residence Inn by Marriott, working at the front desk as well as at their lobby bar as a bartender.

Then for my birthday in early December I was out at the club, sweating my ass off and having a great time with some of my local favorite people, Jon included, of course. I went home to Atlanta for Christmas, and apparently I stopped working at Jon's hotel on December 31st, 2011. Although there's no record of it on Facebook… Happy Birthday, Jon!! Would have been appropriately celebrated around this time. But before we get into 2012…

There was one more thing that happened in 2011, *maybe* very early on in 2012. Jon took a trip to Vegas for a poker tournament. I wasn't invited, but that was okay. We hadn't been away from each other for more than a couple of days during any of the prior turbulence, and now that things had settled down and we were getting along a whole lot better I figured getting some space couldn't be terrible. Plus, I'd started grad school so I had assignments and things that were due. I believe he was going to be gone a week.

When Jon got back, I thought he seemed off. Just generally different. But I didn't know specifically what was up. I did remember what he'd said previously about couples who don't travel together, but I'd figured because it was for a specific tournament it made sense. He told me he was going somewhat at the last minute also. Again, it wasn't so much that I hadn't been included but more about him acting differently now that he was back.

A friend of his had arrived at the house – not one of Jon's poker friends per se but a friend that Jon had for a long time that he'd introduced to online poker. The point is that Leeford wanted to hear about Jon's trip. Now, I realize my next move was a bit crazy, but bear with me. Since I was in grad school and had purchased a recording device to be used for school assignments, I hit record, left it in my bag, left my bag in the room, and (I'm guessing) went out to the pool house to check on my fish.

But sometimes ignorance is bliss…

I probably didn't need to know any of what I learned, but I had a feeling. So, when I listened to Jon and Leeford's conversation play back, hoping it'd just be a waste of time, I found out the following: Jon had two hotel rooms in Vegas (why? I don't know) and had ended up hooking up with three dudes during the time he was out there. He and Leeford were laughing about it with Jon recalling having to stop hooking up and rush to the airport, leaving the final dude in the second room, never checking out of the other (or something like that) because he was going to miss his flight. I have no idea if these were escorts or how he met them, I just knew there were three of them and that he'd had a really great time. No idea how the poker had turned out.

Now, how do you bring up to your boyfriend that you know he cheated on you because you recorded him bragging about it to his buddy? Not sure exactly how I started the conversation, but I told him all of it— that I'd recorded him. I repeated the details so he knew I knew. I think he tried to deny it at first, then he just quit. He didn't try to make me out to be a psycho for recording him, which I think a lot of people would do. But he also didn't apologize, or cop to it. The conversation just fizzled out. The distrust did not. **Loose lips sink ships all the damn time.**

This was the first time I knew that I had been cheated on by anyone. And whether Jon believes this or not, I had not physically cheated on him at this point. And if my ideal partner descriptor had a part two to go along with inspiring me to be a **better man**, it had cheating as an absolute deal-breaker. But did I walk away? Nope.

We'd been monogamous for the beginning of when we were together, then things got hazy but not anything overtly behind each other's backs, then he cheated.

I felt like Jon attached assumptions and meaning to a lot of things. I am truly just a very friendly extroverted person who will talk to anybody who is nice. A bartender at the club and friend of mine was telling Jon what a nice guy I was for getting his jacket back to him, and that somehow gave Jon a bad taste in his mouth. And so in some ways, it became easier to stay isolated; interacting with the outside world seemed to cause problems. Not for me, left to my own devices, but for us. It's sad, too, in retrospect because I used to be the most social person at the bar, and I think that's part of what Jon liked about me at one point. But when being very social comes with consequences, it kind of takes the fun out of it.

> **But your jealousy, oh, I can hear it now**
> **Talkin' down to me like I'd always be around**
> **Pushed my love away like it was some kinda loaded gun**
> **Oh you never thought I'd run**
> -**Better Man**, Taylor Swift

In February of 2012, I got through my second academic residency with grad school and was well on my way to becoming a mental health counselor. Of course, there was still the minor issue of the six hundred hours of supervised counseling I would need before I'd actually get my master's and before I could apply for licensure. Where I was going to get those was still uncertain. However, during the second academic residency, one of my school professors mentioned that the State University could be an option. It was only two hours from where I lived with Jon, and it was apparently a pretty great, student-focused program where it sounded like I could get excellent experience and gain a lot of clinical knowledge. Plus, being a relatively young clinician would likely come with some challenges if I was working with adults of all ages; working with primarily undergrads made a lot of sense. I was older than them to where they wouldn't (hopefully) be questioning my competence, and I had been their age recently enough to have a solid grasp of some of their struggles as undergrads. The more I thought about it, the more this seemed like an excellent opportunity. That was still over a year away but certainly something to think about.

CHAPTER 25

Party Time

I'd be lying if I picked a party, a time or a place where the following happened because in all fairness I have none of those details. But what matters is that this story is absolutely a true account of a hilarious memory from the time Jon and I were together (so sometime between the end of 2009 and 2016 – that's the best I can give you). My very vague recollection wants to say the words "Palm Springs" and "white party", but those are uncorroborated details at best, so it would be better if I just set the scene...

Jon and I had flown somewhere for what was supposed to be an epic circuit party. I really only remember that we entered what was a huge warehouse-style room, music blaring, and plenty of circuit-style gays surrounding the center stage, where the DJ was spinning great music. I couldn't even tell you what Jon and I were on, drug-wise, as we entered the arena...but I could venture to guess ecstasy, "trail mix", and/or GHB may have factored into the equation. So, when we entered the room – on the left side – was a darkened stage, the middle was where the DJ was spinning on his stage with an active crowd devoted to him, and perhaps a third darkened stage on the right side. Again, this was a tremendous warehouse-style or ballroom room with ceilings far taller than any man could reach. It was shaping up to be another really fun night of dancing and debauchery.

I don't even remember if Jon and I did any dancing or if we simply had the brilliant idea of seeing what kind of **trouble** we could get ourselves into from the start. We were high on some variety of club drugs to ensure the night was a blast.

So Jon and I, having arrived in whatever was club-appropriate attire for this particular party, slipped under the stage skirt of the left side stage. We made our way to the center area underneath this particular stage, pushing cardboard boxes out of the way and setting up shop. Once we waited a few seconds to ensure security had not seen us slip under this unoccupied stage, we started taking off our clothes. Dancing is fun and all, but sometimes it just makes more sense to fuck…right? So getting down to it is what we did. And it was hot! Both literally and figuratively; we were sweaty as hell! It was fun in that we could hear the beats of the music the DJ was spinning and the ever-growing crowd in the distance surrounding the center stage. But mostly, we were just focused on each other. We were fucking like animals with the music drowning out any noises or words we may've been exchanging in the moment. **(Words…for just us to know**?) We'd made this space under the stage our own little sex den, and no one was the wiser.

Suddenly there was commotion overhead and what sounded like a stampede rushing in our direction. What had previously been a space where Jon and I could really get into it and not be bothered was suddenly the focal point of the event. Not to mention what had initially seemed like blackout curtains skirting the stage actually proved to be at least partially transparent now that someone was clearly performing and the lights had gone on. And performing, she was! She was singing her heart out, there was clearly dancing going on involving any number of people, and the stage was lit up, brightly. We could see out through the stage's skirt, although I doubt anyone could see us. There was a sea of men pressed up to the barricades surrounding the stage, and it was packed! There was no way of subtly slipping out from under this stage without anyone noticing, especially given that he and I were both butt naked. So we figured waiting it out was our only option.

Then multiple men began reaching their hands under the stages skirt, grabbing at the cardboard boxes that were literally the only thing that was protecting us from being seen by someone in the outside world. But the boxes were not within arm's reach for these guys. As soon as Jon realized what was happening, he started forcefully pushing the boxes from where they were barricading us toward the outstretched hands. As these hands began ripping open the boxes and pulling out Erika Jayne T-shirts and throwing them into the crowd, Jon and I alternated between hastily putting our clothes back on and shoving cardboard boxes at the pairs of hands that continued to appear that were trying to reach for these boxes. All the while, it was clear that Erika Jayne— who neither of us had ever heard of, and who we had no idea was scheduled to do a pop-up— was giving one hell of a performance. She and her backup dancers must've given them quite the show because from under the stage it sounded like a Riverdance-type situation set to club music.

It wasn't until we ran out of boxes to shove and we had gotten ourselves completely clothed that someone stuck their head under the stage's skirt, presumably to check and make sure all of the boxes were opened and all T-shirts had been distributed. I don't think this person even acknowledged us, and if he saw us at all I can only imagine he thought we were part of the crew.

Fortunately, Jon had grabbed us each an Erika Jayne T-shirt before shoving an opened box toward the outstretched hands, at some point. So we each ended up with a souvenir to forever remember this intensely chaotic but hilarious experience.

When the crowd disbursed and Erika was done, Jon and I went outside to get some fresh air. A shirtless man approached us as we were chatting and simply asked, "Oh my gosh, did you see Erika Jayne? Was she not fucking INCREDIBLE!??!" We just laughed uncontrollably…

CHAPTER 26

Police brutality

On March 17, 2012, I was working the three-to-eleven shift out at Shell Island Resort on Wrightsville Beach. I loved working out there and had great colleagues. It was a lot of fun, and I liked having a reputation for going above and beyond for guests. The commute was a long one. The hotel itself and the house downtown were about as far from each other as two points can be while still falling within the New Hanover County geographical area. This wasn't a deterring factor for me, I liked driving just fine. The only problem was that I wasn't supposed to be doing it; my license had been revoked. A .08 DWI caused me to lose it, but I still had to drive to Jacksonville for work. And multiple driving-on-a-suspended-license charges later, here I was. I was headed home from work…on what turned into St. Patrick's Day at the stroke of midnight, although I had not realized that. I was more focused on it being the dog's birthday (the Blackness and Ms. Brownsville, Texas, better known as Blackie and Brownie, two Chihuahuas Jon acquired during our time together that had my heart).

On the drive home, I was headed down MLK Parkway when traffic slowed. Shit. It was a DWI checkpoint, which was fine in the sense that I hadn't been drinking but not great given my license situation. I called Jon, as we were planning to go out to the club since it was a Saturday night and I wanted to give him the heads up. We had a quick chat, then I pulled forward and rolled down my window. I told the officer I didn't have my license, and he asked for my name, date of birth, address, and phone number. I was in my work uniform, name tag and all, that read, "Bruce." The officer went over to his car to punch in my info, then came back and asked me for my info again, so I repeated it. He then informed me that he said he couldn't find me in the system. He stated that because he was unable to locate me in the system, "Sir, you're about five seconds from going to jail right now." I responded, "On what charges?" and he said, "I don't have to have a *reason* to take you to jail. Look around. You're in MY house now!" The officer then essentially bounced me off of his hip into a parked police car and forced me to the ground where in total six officers piled on top of me and cuffed me and everything. I was terrified. I didn't understand what had just happened. Honestly, I still don't to this day. The only additional information I ever gleaned from the police report was that the officer said that I "took a step back," which is why I got "hip-checked," a term I was unfamiliar with but have since come to know.

    I wasn't aware of it at the time, but there was a news crew there filming the checkpoint, so the next day at work everyone was like, "Bruce, I saw you on the news! Are you okay?" I was not. I had to go to the hospital for what I was convinced were broken ribs, but they turned out to be just bruised. One of the worst parts was that when I'd been loaded into the back of the police car I learned that it was this seemingly violent officer that would be taking me everywhere I needed to go for the rest of the night, starting with the hospital. I pleaded with the captain for it to be anyone but him, but it was "his arrest," so he had to see it through. Officer Bobby Ridley and I were stuck together.

    On the way to the hospital, the officer assured me the entire incident was caught on police dashcam video. Oh, thank God! I let him know that he was going to be in trouble if that was the case, given that he escalated a conversation into a violent assault in a matter of seconds. He laughed and promised me we could watch the footage together *in court*. That was fine, I was just glad to hear there was footage.

    The hospital X-rays were fine, the doctor explained that bruised ribs are very painful but that they didn't see any fractures. I was loaded back into the police car and headed to booking, still with the same officer. Officer Butthead started asking me questions about me. I'd already told him on the side of the road that I was headed home from work at Shell Island Resort; the name tag also had the Shell Island logo. I told him I was also in a master's program, to which he let me know I was too stupid to be getting a master's degree. I had not realized we were playing *that* game and that me seeking further education was going to bruise his fragile ego. So I just stopped talking.

At the booking place, he took my wallet and started going through it. He quickly grinned when he pulled out a school ID or something. "Oh, so I see here you gave me your middle name...your first name is Thomas." "Yeah, Thomas is my first name...no one's ever called me that." He responded, "Sorry, I didn't catch that...I couldn't understand you...musta been your lisp." I thought, "Oh my fucking god, what is this, high school?" I'd been arrested by a bully in literally every sense of the word. (I wonder how many kids he hip-checked into lockers in his day...?) I think there were a couple more comments about my lower-than-average, inferior-to-Officer-Butthead's IQ, but whatever.

One thing I failed to mention is that when we went from the hospital to booking, we had to go back through the checkpoint. Officer Butthead said something to his chief about "securing the footage from the dashcam(s)," which apparently must have been code for "make sure to destroy it if it makes me look bad" because when court came, no dashcam footage existed. Also, even though all officers were issued an audio recording device that they were supposed to always have on them, Officer Butthead told the judge that his cell phone was always located where the audio device should be because he and his wife had a five-year-old, so in case his wife called, his phone had to be there instead of this device. And to the judge, that made perfect sense. Jon picked me up from jail. I was glad to see him.

Initially, Jon was just as outraged as I was. I mean, don't get it twisted. I wasn't mad that I got in trouble over not having a license; that was legit. But at the time, I was, like, 130 pounds. A six-officer pin-down led by this narcissistic homophobe of a cop, I believe, sounds like excessive force. And when I say pin down, I mean knees on my back while I can't breathe and I'm trying to inform someone, "You're hurting me," through a face pressed into grass. As for the news footage, the CD they burned for me of the footage was just me in handcuffs; they didn't have any of the takedown (assault). That didn't stop me from filing a complaint with the Office of Professional Standards, but it also made it easy for them to say "unsubstantiated" to my claims. I wrote the mayor, city council members, the news, and anyone I could think of. I was especially irritated over the making-fun-of-me bullshit.

For the record, I do not have, nor have I ever had, a lisp. He could have just as easily called me a faggot. I knew what he meant.

CHAPTER 27

Mean

This was so long ago, but it ultimately created a lot of disconnect between me and Jon. I'll use emails to try and illustrate, as some of our issues here I haven't thought about in a long time.

> **I used to know my place was a spot next to you**
> **Now I'm searching the room for an empty seat**
> **'Cause lately I don't even know what page you're on**
> -The Story of Us, Taylor Swift

Officer Dudley was someone Jon knew who had a position in law enforcement and who was gay too. Jon thought it would be helpful if I spoke with him about what happened. So when Officer Dudley was standing in the driveway one day when I came home, I figured that was why he was there. I had never met him before. Jon hadn't said he'd be there, and Jon wasn't home, but Dudley and I started talking. I figured since Jon had spearheaded this, surely this guy was 'safe.' But when Jon got home shortly thereafter (I likely texted him), it became clear that Jon wished I had known to wait before saying anything (I don't know how I was supposed to know that, but okay). I did get the sense that maybe Officer Dudley had dual loyalties when he mentioned that he'd taken Officer Butthead's sister to prom, back in the day.

> **A simple complication**
> **Miscommunications lead to fallout**
> **So many things that I wish you knew**
> **So many walls up I can't break through**
>   -**The Story of Us**, Taylor Swift

Dudley ended up causing issues for Jon and me in that whatever Dudley shared that day, Jon asked me not to cite Dudley as a source to anyone I spoke to as we'd be burning a good source of info, potentially. Here's an email from Jon, although I don't know what I said that prompted it, and whatever I said must not have been via email as I have no record…

Email sent 3/29/2012 from Jon:

> I have the ability to comprehend and if you were to give me a reasonable explanation of how I have not supported you on the police brutality then you will receive my apologies. From my perspective I have been looking out for your interest from the minute you called me on the phone to let me know you were pulling into a police check point and requested you remain on the line until you cleared it. from sitting by the phone all evening. From going out and searching for you, from paying 1,000 for the privilege of bailing you out of jail. From trying to enlist the help from up until this instance a police officer who had always been helpful in these sort of matters. From being blindsided by your embarrassing admission that you had been intentionally uncooperative with the police in providing your name despite repeated opportunities to disclose this detail to me based on the questions I

asked about the incident right after it happened and again the next day. From trying point out to Dudley that despite the admission of deception that the issued was the brutality. From pointing out to you that I did not think Dudley had your back on this issue and seemed to be advocating for the officer that initiated your arrest keep Dudley. From your dismissal of my single request, to leave Dudley out of the matter. From your rude, ungrateful responses at my attempts to make sure you were considering the potential side effects of your actions, not to talk you out of taking action but to be sure you are armed with as much information for your benefit.

Your rush to cut me off on the issue instead of having some dialog may contribute to your categorizing me as the enemy since shutting me down only leaves you to come up with your own conclusions as to where I may be heading. How my pointing out that the city site on filing complaints states that they will respond in thirty days places me in the enemy camp or in some way is encouraging u not to pursue the abuse charges is beyond me. Ironically, I only know about this fact because of my effort to make sure that you got the information on how to file so you could pursue the matter. The other day when you cut me off I was only trying to make sure you were aware that you may hinder your attorney's ability to defend you and having the charges pleaded down on the resisting arrest if you admit to being guilty of intentionally being deceptive about your identity. The court is unlikely and may be unable to reduce or throw out the charges if you admit to them in a public forum. I was trying to make sure you were aware of this not to discourage you but to make sure you were not saying "I wish I had known that." I think it's healthy to consider the practicalities of your actions even though you have made your decision.

Asking you to keep Dudley anonymous in this matter is in no way a meant as a lack of support to you. the fact of the matter despite my belief he was not acting in your best interest, a point I have no way to prove or disprove, Dudley has been a rich source of information to me over the years and your drawing him into the matter achieves nothing. He was not there and about the only thing you can expect to achieve is ruining a good source of information for me and if called to defend his after the fact discussions with you will certainly point out your reluctant disclosure that you were intentionally hindering Ridley's ability to identify you.

So you're probably right I probably will not ever understand how you came to the conclusion that I have not been supportive.

Jon

Now I'm standing alone in a crowded room
And we're not speaking
And I'm dying to know
Is it killing you like it's killing me? Yeah
I don't know what to say since the twist of fate
When it all broke down
And the story of us looks a lot like a tragedy now
-**The Story of Us**, Taylor Swift

Truly, Dudley tricked me into saying whatever I did about being deceptive, I think. It's this whole complicated mess that rehashing seems pointless to do. It is worth mentioning that Dudley said that whether I gave my first name properly or the name that everyone calls me, my middle name, then the officer absolutely should have been able to find me in the system.

It is also worth mentioning that on the day I went to court, the judge insisted that everyone clear the courtroom for my case. And Jon was not there. Not because he'd been ushered out; he just didn't come. Was this retaliation for me calling him unsupportive? You'd have to ask him. But basically at every step, from talking to Dudley forward, everything I did was wrong. And he let me know it. Anything with a lawyer, from just getting one, to what I did say, and what I didn't say, from not being grateful enough that he'd bailed me out, to not asking enough advice from him. None of it was done the way someone "should" respond in such a situation. My first mistake—speaking candidly with HIS friend who HE had told me to speak with.

> **How'd we end up this way**
> **See me nervously pulling at my clothes and trying to look busy**
> **And you're doin' your best to avoid me**
> **I'm starting to think one day, I'll tell the story of us**
> **How I was losing my mind when I saw you here**
> **but you held your pride like you should've held me**
>
> -**The Story of Us**, Taylor Swift

I was trying to be proactive about making sure my complaint wasn't being ignored. Jon said they'd get back to me within thirty days based on the website. I let him know that the Office of Professional Standards voicemail says someone should make contact in a couple of days once they have been assigned to the case, so it hopefully wouldn't take thirty days. We were both going off different sources of information, but even that created friction.

He'd encouraged me to speak with Dudley only to then tell me he didn't think Dudley was working in my best interest. It was hard to feel supported when that's how this kicked off.

I'll admit, I didn't do a whole lot to keep the peace with Jon. His email above was met with gems like this.

Email from me to Jon, 3/29/2012:

> If some1 helped dick u over I wouldnt ask u to keep it a secret. guess thats where we differ.

I followed up shortly thereafter with this:

> Jon, your asking me to keep Dudley out of conversations with my lawyer or WECT came on the heels of Dudley manipulating me to benefit the officer that I was assaulted by. Asking me to walk on egg shells to avoid getting on your "friends" bad side is NOT having my back. realizing that hes getting what he signed up for if I use his name when retelling what happend seems like an appropriate response from a boyfriend of almost 3 years...do u not see that? how about a little anger at him seeing as how he played u 4 a fool!?!?

Admittedly I knew trying to make Jon feel wrong by saying he was played for a fool was not the most tactful of moves. It was a well-cemented fact in my mind that Jon could not get on board with the idea that he'd done anything wrong, ever. But I said it. I should have known if my intent was to get him back on my side and mad at someone other than myself, this was hardly the best play...

Jon wrote back the following email:

> >Twist it however you want Bruce. If you have a way of proving that Dudley conspired against you and I can help you verify that as

fact then why wouldn't you say so before now. Will verification of Dudley's assisting or advising Ridley in his report prove that you did not physically resist arrest when Ridley went to handcuff you? I think you knowledge yourself that the video is the only evidence that will prove excessive force was used. Your attorney is subpoenaing any video that has any footage of the incident according to what you have said to me. why wouldn't you wait to see the video before charging on recklessly without any legal counsel. Your attorney could identify the other officers in the photo if no video is produced and subpoena them. He may be able to crack one of them into admitting they were being overkill. Your marking up a police incident report with what you say are untruths holds no weight in court. You being mad as hell over how you were mistreated by Ridley will not make charges stick in court. They will show that you are an admitted lire and that your version of what happened cannot be trusted. Them physically restraining you and your hindering their ability to identify you are one and the same charge. In other words they could have and may have charged you with resisting arrest even if it was only a matter of you putting your hands behind your back and getting in the squad car without anything physical. Your admission that you were intentionally hindering Ridley's ability to identify you could possibly result in the charge of resisting arrest stick regardless of the outcome of the excessive force charge. Proving excessive force would likely result in them dropping the cell phone charges.

    >The bottom line is there are a host of considerations that you and I may not be qualified

to address that should be. You have chosen your go it alone approach and placed me in the enemy camp which is hurtful, wrong and paranoid. You run the risk of doing more harm than good letting your emotions manage your actions but I have been in situations like your where I have let emotions drive the bus so I understand even if I disagree with your approach. I don't think I have ever been so dismissive of someone who has only tried to help. If I received the anything close to level of support on anything that I have shown you on this matter they would receive nothing but my deepest appreciation. Instead you intentionally do not discuss my request to keep Dudley out of an incident he wasn't involved in when it happened (hardly walking on egg shells. It was not as if he was a witness to the incident and I asked you to leave him out). you disclose what you believe to be collusion between Dudley and Ridley on what appears in the incident report. An allegation that you now state you have evidence to prove but have never stated up until last night that you had (and have still not stated what that evidence is). Do you know whether or not Even if you were to prove they colluded on the incident would that be a violation of police policy? You do not dispute anything in the incident report that you said to Dudley. In fact you are saying that he repeated your version of what happened. That is why you think it was collusion because the statements you made to Dudley are too accurately reflected in the police report. Or the officers reflection of what took place too conveniently answer statements made to Dudley. You are not alleging that anything Dudley may have reported to Ridley is not what you said you are alleging that Ridley's responses to those statement were untrue. I think you will agree that you would have a tough time believing the story too if the shoe was on someone else's foot. "yes your honor I was trying to avoid arrest by not disclosing my true identity but other than that I was being totally cooperative I was just standing there limp noodle totally cooperating with police when five cops jumped on me threw me to the ground"

>At any rate I feel like I am owed just a little consideration in all of this. Your lack of humility and consideration for anyone but yourself is appalling. Even after letting me scream at Dudley in your defense only to have you admit moments later that you were being intentionally deceptive about how the events unfolded at the check stop. Instead of apologizing to me you just compound your lies by saying that you told me about it when clearly you did not. It is not an insignificant fact that I would have missed had you told me. you leave me standing there stunned by a up until then undisclosed admission based on similar questioning by me that makes me look like a fool and you a lire in the eyes of Dudley. Is it possible that Dudley came over in good faith but your admission turned his opinion toward the cop? Unlikely because he seemed fairly certain that you were withholding fact based on his questions. Can you blame him for thinking you may be distorting the facts regarding the brutality charges?

>You may consider also that you are still driving without a license and carrying paraphernalia in your car and do not need any undue attention. This would boast the argument for taking the slow approach and file charges after

you get a paper license. Should you get picked up for revoked they may search your car and if evidence is found they may search your home (and mine) and we are not practicing choir over here. You can continue your go it alone approach and keep me on the side of the enemy but I would appreciate it if you would at least keep in mind that I have two alcohol licenses that would be jeopardized by any charges against me and I cannot afford to make enemies with anyone at the police department. And you may have unnecessarily ruined a contact already for me I just hope you have not created an enemy… if that matters to you

He makes some good points clearly but not the ones about the moment when he felt I had lied. I maintain that Dudley trapped me into this moment where I lost Jon's support, seemingly. When Jon started saying I'd made him an enemy or moved him into the enemy camp, all I really wanted was for him to admit that he'd invited an enemy into our camp because he literally did. Jon wasn't being made to be an enemy. He just started to make this about him, at least from my perspective.

> **I liked it better when you were on my side**
> **The battle's in your hands now**
> **But I would lay my armor down**
> **If you'd say you'd rather love than fight**
> **-The Story of Us**, Taylor Swift

There is nothing more that I wanted and needed at this moment than a fucking hug from my boyfriend.
But instead…

> **I'm scared to see the ending**
> **Why are we pretending this is nothin'?**

**I'd tell you I miss you, but I don't know how
I've never heard silence quite this loud**
			-**The Story of Us**, Taylor Swift

I responded with...

Yeah it would help tremendously! proving officer Ridley lied in his account of what happend shows hes capable lying. he recalled the entire course of events to the magistrate at jail. that version of events didnt include ANY of the things Dudley added in. All of the things that I dispute from the report were the exact things that Dudley said when he was at home 4 his surprise visit, and u & I were the only 1s there. All Ud have to do is say exactly what Dudley said (the truth) to discredit officer ridley. if his entire report is lies its conceivable that I never physically resisted arrest! so by stating that I need to go out of my way to keep Dudleys name out of this its hurting my case…theres no spin on that.

And he came back with...

How does my confirming that the conversation between Dudley me and you prove that Ridley is lying about anything. It doesn't even prove that Dudley gave details if our conversation to ridley. Details on the magistrates written statement finding there were ground to hold you on the charges made by Ridley are not inconsistent with his arrest report. The arrest report is just more detailed. If I am wrong I would like you to give me how's our testimony pointing out the many points in the arrest report are the same points you raised with Dudley would show that Ridley lied about his version of the events. And again there may be nothing illigal about the Dudley turning over information about our conversation. He is after all a detective.

I am guilty of bringing Dudley into this, and by now I guess you probably think I'm conspiring with Ridley and Dudley, but the fact is I did it to help you. The fact that it was a bad descion I accept responsibility for that, however having always benifited from his advise or information in the past i did not consider he would not do likewise here.

Your disregard for my request is just outright betrayal against me even if u were able to gain anything from it, but then again I would have never asked u to leave him out of it if that were the case anyway. So say whatever makes you feel justified in your actions but I'm gonna say that u know u were wrong and your pride wont let u admit it. I also feel confidant that your refusal to discuss your intention s because "you don't want me to try and change your mind" is evidence that somewhere inside u you had some uncertainty whethrr what u were going to do was the right course of action. I can't imagine that u fully discussed any of this with ur lawyer and he told u that Dudley had any bearing on the case. It really makes me sad you hold me on so low regard that you can't trust me, talk to me and are willing to dismiss my request the way you have without so much as asking why. I imagine it feels alot like the violation of trust u must of felt from Ridley when he thew I to the ground and jumped on top of u without without offering you an opertunity explain why u should mot be arrested or to clarify your true identity.

At this point, I wish he would have just said, "No, I will not do these things, even if they would be helpful to you," because these long manipulative emails where he plays the victim are the last thing I needed following what really was a traumatic assault.

> **This is looking like a contest**
> **Of who can act like they care less**
> **But I liked it better when you were on my side**
>   -**The Story of Us**, Taylor Swift

I responded with this:

> Not the arrest report, the recorded statement he gave the magistrate where he recalls the arrest. he adds about 3 times of me insisting im Bruce in the Dudley version

Then I sent this:

> Much like the officers incident report your email becomes unreadable about half way thru. u think I should wait to act on any of this? we are leaving for 20 days and my court date is 2 days after we get back! if "letting my emotions drive the bus" is the reason i walked to Bess street yesterday then its a good thing they r bcuz thats how I got a Sgt. assigned to my case. not acting will get me no where! and if u cant see why Id b frustrated that you are more concerned about Dudley than me getting justice then perhaps you arent on my team after all. if Dudley is the enemy then y is he your concern? u brought him into this then he helped to discredit me by falsifying a report on an event that, like u said, he wasnt there to witness.

I think Jon gets "animated" by this because I did get a little forward movement in my case by being persistent after he'd been essentially telling me **you need to calm down**. But here's his response (which is my previous email but with his thoughts interjected):

>Much like the officers incident report your email becomes unreadable about half way thru. u think I should wait to act on any of this? Ur charges of police brutality happened 10 days ago. Your attorny will certainly continue the Case if he plans on introducing any of your counter charges into the case assuming your using one. I'm pretty sure ur not acting on any advise from council currently. we are leaving for 20 days and my court date is 2 days after we get back! if "letting my emotions drive the bus" is the reason i walked to Bess street yesterday then its a good thing SO WHAT UR SAYING IS THAT U WOULD NOT HAVE BEEN HEARD IF U WOULD HAVE WAITED FOR YOUR ATTORNY TO PURSUE THIS MATTER? THE LTHER DAY U SAID IT WAS IN THE HANDS OF YOUR ATTORNY, they r bcuz thats how I got a Sgt. assigned to my case. not acting will get me no where! and if u cant see why Id b frustrated that you are more concerned about YYOUR MAKING STATEMENT THAT I AM MORE CONCERNED ABOUT DUDLEY THAN YOU ARE BASED ON NOTHI NG BUT YOUR OWN PARANOID THOUGHTS. I HAVE E PLAINED TO YOU WHY I MADE THE REQUEST AND AM WAITING FOR YOU TO SHOW ME THAT TO DO SO WOULD JEPARDIZE YOUR CASE AGAINST RIDLEY. Dudley than me getting justice then perhaps you arent on my

team after all. PERHAPS IM NOT ON YOUR SIDE MAY E CORRECT BECAUSE YOUR UNWILLINGNESS TO DISCUSS ANY OR LISTEN TO ANYTHING I SAY AND YOUR RECKLESS DISREGARD OF ANYTHING I HAVE TO SAY MAKES ME UNCERTAIN THAT YOU WILL NOT SCREW UP YOUR CASE AND MAKE THINGS ONLY WORSE FOR YOURSELF, I DON'T SEE ANY REASON TO GET IN FRONT OF A MOVING BUS WITH U IF YOU FEEL THE Way u do toward me. Why should I. That doesn't mean I don't beleive you were mistreated by Ridley either because I do. Dudley is not my enemy in general just on this issue.

Suggested listen: "**Bulletproof**," "**White Horse**," "**Forever & Always**," and "**You're Not Sorry**." Aah, fuck it. Listen to **Taylor's Version** of the *Fearless* **CD** all the way through. It's always a good idea.

My final response to Jon on March 30, 2012:

How have I disregarded everything uve said? when all u do is play devils advocate its almost impossible to decipher what you are saying, what u r suggesting, and what you are just asking questions about. my attorney is handling my charges only. i think i mentioned already that getting him to play prosecutor would be 20–30k. when all is said and done my number 1 goal is to feel like Ive been heard. That doesnt happen by waiting around, and waiting around makes me more angry

So many things that you wish I knew
But the story of us might be ending soon
-**The Story of Us**, Taylor Swift

At the time that this was going on, I described what I was dealing with—trying to get the word out about what had happened and how unreasonable I felt it was—by saying I felt like I was screaming in the middle of a crowded room and no one was listening or paying attention to me. "**The Story of Us**" is so fitting because the person who I needed on my side the most was not. And the references to crowded rooms just felt too fitting to not include in clips throughout that explanation.

On April 5, Jon sent a response that would've stirred all of these things up again…then he realized he was responding to my email from five days ago…so we didn't kick it back up…

Suggested listen: "**Mr. Perfectly Fine.**"

Finally, that exchange of emails was OVER! Thank goodness because Jon and I need to start packing for our trip to go see his nephew in Madagascar. It felt important to show the intense exchanges we were hurling back and forth just before jetting off to a foreign country.

Sidebar: Officer Ridley is still listed as a police officer on the police department's website. It doesn't look like he's been promoted, as far as I can tell. Not sure what he's doing with his life other than being a family man. But I was curious to see if there was any reason to believe he'd gotten any anger management or anything that suggested he was a nicer person these days…I'll let whoever may read this decide. Here's a Facebook post from August of 2022, almost exactly ten years after the incident, that Officer Ridley typed up and posted…just to illustrate the type of person I was assaulted by if that wasn't already clear:

> I do not pay taxes to support illegal aliens with cell phones and free medical insurance, I do not pay taxes so our incompetent president can pay off others student debt, or any portion of

their dept. There are millions who have worked their entire life, paid into social security, and are expected to live on average $1600 a month. SO TIRED OF THE BULLSHIT!!!!!

So yeah, that's him, in a nutshell.

So our trip to Madagascar begins with a flight from where we lived to New York. As always, Jon has packed all of the necessities, including glass meth pipes he's decorated with glue-on googly eyes and colorful pipe cleaners to ensure they make it through customs and to our final destination. I could not make this shit up if I wanted to…I'm guessing the meth was in an underwear pouch by his balls when we were on the flight, but I can't remember which method he used to carry it for this trip with any certainty…I know that it made it though.

CHAPTER 28

Welcome to New York

Our trek to Madagascar included an initial flight to New York, where our only plans while we were there were to have dinner with Barton. Barton and Brantley had long since broken up, but Jon and Barton had been friends for a long time and NY was Barton's home base. The back story on Barton is that although he seemed to enjoy making me uncomfortable when I first met him— talking about watching Brantley getting fucked and things I really didn't want to hear about— he had since quit trying to make me squirm in his presence. I think he had also responded to something I posted somewhere about the whole police incident, something supportive, publicly, and so that was appreciated. We were only going to be in New York overnight before we hopped our flight to get to the island of Madagascar the next day.

Dinner with Barton was short-lived. Barton brought up the police incident to get an update as to where things were with that, and somewhere into the discussion Jon got pissed and started calling me a liar, repeatedly, loudly, in this restaurant. Yelling and screaming are too strong of words, but he was shouting, and this was a small table, and there's no amount of New York noise that justified this. And nothing new came up in this conversation; apparently this was just pent-up rage coming from Jon. It is worth noting that somewhere along the way in our relationship, I began asking Jon, "Why are you raising your voice at me?" I am a strong believer that there's nothing that is going to get resolved more easily if people are yelling and screaming, something I'm sure I learned from watching my mom in action as a kid. And while I didn't say this phrase to Jon at this moment, I am confident I did not raise my voice. I just got up and walked out.

Fortunately, I have friends that live in New York. I went and found Nolan and Timmy, a couple I had known for years. I met Nolan in my beachside college town when he was working at Starbucks as a barista and he knew my name before I gave it. I thought this was creepy, no matter how hot he was…then he posted on my Myspace wall, "All I have to say is white mocha." Also, a creepy-ass way to say hello. Nolan is literally hands down far and away the best sex I've ever had. And that night I got to fuck both he and Timmy, so it was like double the fun. Their New York apartment was some-number-of-floors up and their bedroom windows were open. There were people on the street laughing after I came because I can be very loud, and Nolan didn't put the pillow over my face like I told him to. I miss those guys…

CHAPTER 29

Surviving Madagascar

Internally I was very much on the fence about leaving the country for an African island when Jon and I were barely on speaking terms. But the tickets were booked, and I just kind of went with it and hoped for the best. We were going to Madagascar because his nephew was in the Peace Corps and was helping a remote village to dig latrines. We weren't expected to participate in the buckets of fun that this sounded like it must be or anything, although there were parts of the trip that were less enjoyable than this activity probably would have been. To be clear, any misconception that this was to be a "vacation" faded fast. From the start, Jon and I weren't speaking, and it was beginning to look like—even though we were no longer in the US—we'd be going our separate ways for the twenty-day excursion. His sister, Paula, was meeting us there; and of course his nephew, Ted, was already living the ungroomed life he'd signed up for.

I was in my online master's program and had given both of my professors the heads-up that I'd be out of the country for this time period. Based on the guidebook Jon had purchased, Wi-Fi existed and shouldn't be too much of an issue when it came to turning in assignments and making weekly discussion posts. I learned the hard way that sometimes guide books lie.

The first night hotel, the Hotel Paon d'or in Antananarivo, was looking like it was going to be my home for twenty days. Jon and Paula were at a different hotel…one that apparently had Wi-Fi. **Mine** did not. Fuck. I had to make nice with Jon to turn in a school assignment. And that's how I rejoined the pack and began the "vacation" of a lifetime.

I was fortunate enough to have visited Africa before. My mom is a travel agent and she took my brother, my sister, and me to South Africa, Botswana, and Zambia. We went out on safari and saw all kinds of Lion King characters in their natural habitat. We stayed in very nice luxury lodges and resorts. Madagascar was NOT that kind of trip.

Ted (Jon's nephew) had tried his best to book an enjoyable adventure while we were in the country. Ted had been living in one of the more remote locations offered by the Peace Corps, digging latrines and letting go of concepts like personal hygiene. (I say that kiddingly; he's a super nice guy, and he didn't smell…well, I didn't notice it. Aunt Paula had to room with him, so she may say otherwise.) Some of the highlights of this trip include (**blank space**).

Some of the more difficult parts to contend with were: When our Jeep got stuck in the mud on the way to see…something…we never got to see it, so I can't even remember what it was. Heat, horseflies, and an immovable vehicle for most of that day. On the trip, Jon got sick (Dave Matthews made a really good point when he sang "Don't Drink the Water"…or even brush your teeth with it, apparently). I know I mentioned the Wi-Fi already, but as a follow-up, I failed career counseling because Madagascar didn't have much of any reliable Wi-Fi at the time we were there, so turning in assignments was an impossibility. (When I retook it I got an A, so it was just a waste of tuition money and time.) What else…what else…oh! In the US, we've been spoiled by the concept of recycling. In Madagascar they burn tires in the villages, so if you don't like the smell of burning tires, this may not be your destination of choice. You can also walk the beaches where you will find plastic bags or parts of plastic bags that have washed ashore with dead sea life interspersed with litter. We were told that people defecate in plastic bags, tie them up, then throw them in the ocean. Given the sea life situation…that tracks. Oh, and if you've never seen an actual wall covered in bugs when the sun goes down, and that happens to be on your bucket list, Madagascar is your country.

The nicest part of Madagascar (other than leaving) was Nosy Beach. The place where we stayed on Nosy Beach was operated by a French couple, and hearing his sister, Paula, speak to the couple in French at meals aggravated Jon, so even that part of the trip had its issues. (Sidenote: In Buenos Aires I watched as Jon said the word "laundry" about twenty times to someone who clearly didn't speak English, as if by saying the word repeatedly the person was going to learn English and then point him in the right direction without any additional hints or gestures. I'm glad I was there to help, if for no other reason so this Spanish-speaking woman didn't have to hear the word "laundry" barked in her face any more times.)

On the trip, Jon and I got along well, and if nothing else at least we had each other to forever cherish our memories of this once-in-a-lifetime excursion.

A funny story (maybe not "funny hahaha" but about as funny as things got in Madagascar): Jon made one slight error in judgment when he gave one of the village kids a piece of candy. He was then mauled; suddenly all the village children circled him as they chanted, "Bonbon! Bonbon!" That was amusing.

It's a really funny trip to remember once you're no longer living it.

> **You always knew how to push my buttons**
> **You gave me everything and nothing**
> **This mad, mad love makes you come running**
> **To stand back where ya stood**
> **I wish you would, I wish you would**
>   -**I Wish You Would**, Taylor Swift

Worth noting: I told my mom we were going to Madagascar "for, like, two weeks," thinking that was sufficient information. It was more like a twenty-day trip. So at some point when my mom couldn't get ahold of me, she called the local police in my area and sent them to my apartment. What she didn't realize was that I'd sublet my apartment to that lovely couple that didn't like background checks. So the police went and banged on the door of my old apartment, where, of course, I had not lived for a very long time. It goes without saying, people who don't like background checks generally aren't big fans of unannounced visits from law enforcement.

The tenants were able to explain they knew nothing about my trip to Africa, given that we didn't know each other like that, and eventually I got word back to the States that I had not been kidnapped.

CHAPTER 30

Superman

The sublet people and I did have a brief discussion about their interactions with the police officer who came looking for me. They had resolved me being "missing" with the police, and as far as I could tell, there was no further issue. But then they stopped paying rent, and I could not track them down to get the rent check, which they typically just brought downtown to the house once a month. I probably let it slide for a month and just paid it myself, thinking they would resurface. But when the next month rolled around and I still could not find them, Jon and I went to investigate. I still had a key to the apartment, so when no one answered, we let ourselves in.

The place was an absolute disaster. Their stuff was all still there, furniture included, but it was a mess. And it was hot. And…there were needles on the floor. It seemed the tenants had fled, and as far as we could tell, the power had been cut off as well. We started poking around. Curious me I went over to the freezer and opened it up. If you think a wall in Madagascar that's covered in bugs sounds gross, I will tell you right now that a freezer full of maggots is so much worse.

I could not contain myself I was so grossed out. Thank goodness Jon was there! He just told me to take the car, go back to the house, and that he would take care of it. He packed up all of the tenants' things (minus the needles) and transported them downtown and put them in storage in his garage. He cleaned out the maggot-infested freezer (I'm guessing?). My point is he saved the day. I could not have handled any of that on my own, at all. And he took care of it, like a boss.

Eventually the couple resurfaced, insisting they get their stuff back. I told them what Jon had told me to say, which was that absolutely they could have their stuff as soon as they paid the rent that I was owed. She was the primary person I'd spoken with each month when they'd drop off the check. She found this to be unreasonable and called me a "faggot." When I spoke with her boyfriend, he was quick to throw her under the bus, insisting that she was the junkie; meanwhile, he was just a college student who didn't do heroin. They had someone call my phone pretending to be law enforcement. I didn't back down, and it wasn't long before they simply stopped calling. They knew how much they owed, and I guess they needed their money for other, more important things.

*Suggested listen: **This Is Why We Can't Have Nice Things**, Taylor Swift

And that's why Jon was my superman.

On July 27, 2012, I sent Jon an email that said, "Come catch me doing something wrong…I wanna be in trouble." I can only guess that meant I had set up the sling in his office.

I'm speculating we got along well for the next month or so… then…

On September 6, 2012, I sent an email to Jon that said:

> Jon,
>
> I will let the police thing go because you are asking me to and for that reason alone. I don't feel like anyone should be treated the way I was that evening—by law enforcement or by anyone else—and I don't think I should just get over it because the video disappeared. I hope no one else in is mistreated by this police department, and I especially hope that it doesn't happen again

because I *finally* shut my mouth about it rather than keep making a stink til someone recognizes that it was NOT ok and takes appropriate action so it doesn't happen again. So here's the deal I'll make with you: if you DO NOT bring it up anymore, neither will I—either in front of you or behind your back. But I'm not going to pretend that after 3 years with someone it doesn't hurt to see how easily you back down, just in the interest of what others may think. Part of me wonders if you're not already out spreading the word about how I'm "crazier than Rob himself" as part of your farewell package.

So that's it. I think I'm officially having the worst day of my life. But I'll just keep that to myself—wouldn't want to burden you with any more "feelings."

If you've got a response, make sure it has nothing to do with this issue. If you want this to be closed, like I said, don't mention it anymore. Peace

B

That email was super passive-aggressive. Actually I'd go so far as to say that email sounded a bit like Axis II…also, very bossy. Jon did not write back. He probably should've said, "Pack your things…get out." LOL. I could be a brat sometimes.

> **Hey it's on me, in my head**
> **I'm the one who burned us down**
> **But it's not what I meant**
> **Sorry that I hurt you**
> **I don't wanna do, I don't wanna do this to you**
> **I don't wanna lose, I don't wanna lose this with you**
> -Afterglow, Taylor Swift

Every year, the first weekend in June, there is an event that is exactly as it sounds—One Magical Weekend. An Orlando hotel hosts a whole bunch of gays and it is a blast! There are other neighboring hotels where people stay as well, but for the most part, it's the main host hotel where you want to be. They have pool parties all day, there's an off-site party each night, and then there's the after-party. So basically, circuit music and go-go boys at various locations around the Disney area, and guys in Speedos for days.

The first evening party each year is Typhoon Lagoon. There are water rides, a lazy river, and a beach area with a man-made tidal wave. They have multiple DJs spinning throughout the weekend and it's always great music.

June of 2013 was the first time I attended One Magical Weekend, and again, this was one of those "Whoa! This is amazing!" kind of trips. So many guys, and everyone is typically very friendly. So yeah, tons of fun. We were there with friends but of course had our own hotel room.

Typhoon Lagoon was a blast, but there's only so much you can do while you're there…right? Okay, I'm bullshitting; you can be completely entertained the entire time you're there without sneaking off to some secluded bushes to have sex. But Jon and I were bored, and those bushes were calling our names. Did I mention we were on Molly? Well, now I have…

Anyway, everyone arrives in clothes with their Speedo underneath, so there are lockers and a key system and all of that good stuff. Unfortunately, when you go have sex behind some random bushes and you lose your locker key, it's only then that you realize that this huge park area has tons and tons of bushes, all of which look the same. So despite our best efforts to recover that key, it was a lost cause. Lesson learned? While you can get handsy on the lazy river like everyone else, don't go fuck in the bushes. You're bound to lose something and all the bushes look the same. And yes, someone let us into our locker, but Jon did have to pay a lost key fee. Oh, and while we were standing in the lost key line or whatever it's called, I turned around and almost said, "Hey!" to the familiar-looking guys in line behind me. Then I had to remember, "Bruce, you know those porn stars, but they do not know you." Although I'm sure if I had said, "You look awfully familiar," they would have laughed.

The next lesson I learned came the next day at the pool party. Jon and I were walking around and there just so happened to be a big table of fruit. As a joke and with Jon's encouragement, I put a banana in my Speedo. And wouldn't you know it? Not even thirty seconds later, there was a very attractive guy with muscles who suddenly wanted to get to know me better. Jon and I have laughed about that quite a bit. So the lesson learned that day was: if you want to make friends at circuit parties, give the illusion that you have a tremendous penis. Guaranteed success.

It's hard to believe that just two months after One Magical Weekend I was moving to Raleigh to begin my internship at a university counseling center. Nine months away from Jon felt reasonable, it wasn't like I'd be in Raleigh forever; nevertheless, I am certain I started being distant. The closer it got to my move date, the more I avoided interacting. After all, *I hate goodbyes*! I always have. If I can get away with it, I'll just leave without having to say it, even if it's rude. But this was not going to be one of those times. Jon was going to help with the U-Haul and everything. He was coming up with me to drop me and the furniture off. The dogs were coming too!

As for what this was going to mean for "us", just about all options were a possibility. Everything from us breaking up to discussions about how long it would take for Jon to sell off his businesses and move up there too (he said it would take a year, so for a nine-month internship telling him to get that ball rolling didn't make much sense). And since nothing was officially decided but all options were on the table, the fact that I was pushing him away was not doing us any favors.

We got up to Raleigh just in time for me to get my keys before the office closed to my sight-unseen apartment. The dogs rode with me while Jon was coming just a bit behind us in the U-Haul. I had to run to the grocery store to get a cashier's check while the impatient apartment lady was trying to get off work. (Jon and I never were very timely.) And when I walked into my new apartment with the dogs, kicked off my flip-flops, and realized the carpet was crusty underneath my feet, I knew at that moment that I had made a huge mistake. But what was I going to do? The office was closed and Jon was not trying to get stuck in Raleigh, he just wanted to unload the furniture and maybe stay the night, but ultimately not go apartment hunting with a packed U-Haul. And so that's where I lived. Jon arrived, and we unpacked. All was situated.

It seemed like we were relatively on the same page; breaking up made sense. We could reevaluate post internship or whatever. Not closing any doors…and we were relatively on the same page with that.

But then we had sex.

I flipped the script on him and decided we had to be together, and I'd been a fool for pushing him away. I committed to coming to see him on weekends and fighting for this relationship. Jon, being relatively unemotional and unaffected as per usual, had his typical "whatever you wanna do" attitude. So yeah, that's how we ended up continuing to trudge along, trying to get this love thing back on track. (You see what being dickmatized can do? If he hadn't stuck around for more sex, he could've had his freedom! LOL.)

> **Never a clean break, no one here to save me**
> **You're the only thing I know like the back of my hand**
>
> **And I can't breathe without you, but I have to**
> -**Breathe**, Taylor Swift

CHAPTER 31

I Think He Knows

In an attempt to surprise Jon with a birthday present I'd worked really hard on, I drove the two hours from my apartment in Raleigh to my former residence with Jon. And wouldn't you know it, the surprise was on me! He'd just gotten finished fucking some dude who had just left. The kicker? He and Kris were tag-teaming the dude! I came in to find them both in their underwear in the house, looking bewildered with guilty smiles.

Jon always hated surprises. I guess maybe I should start hating them too…?

January 5th, 2014, Jon wrote:

> Bruce,
>
> Let me back up a little to try and explain where I thought things were with us or at least where I was with us. Communication between us has been a problem from the beginning of our relationship. I'm not assigning any blame here but for whatever reason engaging in matters of substance between you and I often ends abruptly and/or with no understanding or resolution. I assume you know what I am talking about since you have on many occasions raised the issue yourself or have

used it as a reason not to share information that would normally be discussed by partners.

This lack of communication often leaves both of us to make assumptions about where things are between us based on the actions of the other. I have grown to accept this way of operating. It helps keep our day to day relationship uncomplicated and reduce the conflict between us however I think it comes at a cost to intimacy, passion, understanding, trust and friendship.

This is where I thought things where with us: We are still together. You are living in Raleigh and I expected you were doing your own thing up there. I do not/did not think you were out getting your dick sucked every night but I certainly didn't think you were being as virtuous as you stated in your text to me last night. I was not having regular sex or sex parties down here but have not been totally abstinent either. I had made up my mind that I would not try to pry into what you may or may not be doing and just try to enjoy the time we have together and just see where the relationship goes. This casual approach which I thought you had adopted as well was the result a lot of different things, the main one being your moving to Raleigh. Your announcement that you were moving to charlotte, Atlanta, or Raleigh came when we were having some trouble in our relationship. I feel like had you not been on probation that you would have likely moved sooner and that we would have probably been done by now. The rush to move seemed to die down for a while and things were better but not great between us. I'm guessing several months or more past before Pete and then from Jackie both unknowing told me not only that you were moving but that you were moving in august or September. When I asked you about it you said it was easier to not tell me some stuff because I would create an issue over it or something like that. I took that to mean you just wanted to get out of here without a bunch of goodbyes. So I decided I would honor your desire to keep me out of the loop and was convinced it was pretty much over between us at that point and that maybe we could at least maintain a friendship and that I was going to make the transition for you as easy as possible. We never discussed what our relationship was going to be after the move one time the entire summer which further solidified my belief that you were just ready to move on. Even on the day we moved you up to Raleigh I believed we were on the same page and because I had the past several months to prepare for this day and the fact that I believed we were still going to be good friends I felt pretty good when I headed back home. Only then (you may have said something right when I was leaving the apartment too) did get your note explaining that the move was not intended as a means to break up and that you were still committed to the relationship. The note totally threw me for a loop and frankly I thought the note came from someone who is understandably suffering a case of nervous uncertainty about a pretty big life change. None of your actions up until that point had suggested there was any desire stay together. there was nothing said about breaking up either however the act of moving to another city essentially suggest a breakup in the absence of sharing a desire to remain connected. So I have been taking the relationship one day at a time and just seeing where it goes but have not been sweating it. Fast forward… Since you have been in Raleigh I would say that things have been better between us than they have the last few years of our relationship. There are some of the old problems that come out in the communication department but I think less than before. The fact that we see less of each other may contribute to that improvement rather than it being the result of better communication.

When you asked me in Raleigh if I had been messing around I was taken a little off guard and when you said that you had been totally good. When you asked me if there was someone that I slept with that may have passed gonorrhea I told you that there was nobody that I could have been with that you would not have been exposed to as well and as it turned out neither of us had been exposed to it. When you pressed About my fidelity I gave the same answer that you had given me. I was sort of surprised you asked the question and had declared your celibacy because up until then I felt like we were not talking about what we may or may not have done. I don't know why other people lie about their transgressions but I do it to avoid causing unnecessary pain for, in this case, some meaningless sexcapade I may have had. I firmly believed you had been doing your own thing for a variety of reasons that I will not get into with you. I take you at your word that you have not done anything but keep in mind you have played this card before only to be presented with evidence to the contrary.

I want to finish by saying that I am sorry for what happened again and my details of where I thought things were is an explanation and not an excuse for my behavior.

So where do we go from here.

On January 6th, 2014, I responded to Jon with the following email (1:10 a.m.):

Jon,

I apologize for being really terrible when it came time to let you in on my plans about moving. As I read over your email it became apparent that your perception of what was going on with me was quite accurate, whether I was explaining it to you along the way or not. There are 2 factors regarding my move that I need to add to what you said so that you get the full picture. The first of which is that our town and it's surrounding area does not have the opportunity I needed to get experience as a practicing counselor without (at least) a Master's degree. Period. My realization that I needed to look outside of our area became clear when I realized I was just about done with all of the required course work and the only thing left was the 700 hours [of supervised counseling practice that I needed] spaced out over 3 quarters. Any ideas about the possibility of moving to Charlotte were on the table because my cousins Will and David live there and because it's a much more appealing place to live (in my opinion) than Raleigh. However, my #1 reason for moving anywhere was always school-related, and that's why I ended up in Raleigh, because the program I am in is so perfectly tailored to what I need to (finally) get my MS in Mental Health Counseling.

Now back to the perceptions you mentioned that were right-on...Yes, my announcement that I was moving did come at a time when things were not going well with us. And you are right, had I not been on probation I would have moved during that time period because not being able to talk to someone you live with and should be able to share your life with is unbearable. If you recall, I came to Raleigh for an interview with the counseling center administrators during the time when things were not going well…reflecting on your account, you said there was a time when things got better - and they did, I agree (*in large part because I held firm boundaries of things we would not be talking about and we kept things superficial…I'll come back to this in a second…) and then you heard from Jackie and Pete that I was moving. That's because after a long waiting period (I knew the date they'd let me know by, so I expected it to be long…) I found out I got the internship I'd driven to Raleigh for many months before. By the time I found out, things between us had gotten better. I knew it was going to be harder to move out than it would've been had I gone sooner, but I also knew that no matter what, this opportunity was not one I could pass up - I didn't do a few years of extra school work so that I could work at Shell Island for the rest of my life…

Now back to what I mentioned earlier that I said I'd get back to…You must think I like controlling what you can and can't talk about, or that topics "of substance" are beyond my conversational capabilities or something at this point and I don't blame you. That's not it at all. I, like you, have just come to accept that steering clear of anything personal is just better for our relationship. Why? (and I've tried to explain this before…get ready for the blame game…) I do not get what I need from you on that level. What

I need is and has always been A BOYFRIEND. What I get from you and have never wanted or needed is a father. A boyfriend will listen to you vent and when you're done saying it out loud you can say "thanks for listening." You, on the other hand, give direct advice about exactly what I need to do, step-by-step, and then expect me to do as I'm told. If I don't do what you suggest, you make sure to let me know I'm wrong... If I do take your advice and it doesn't work out, somehow it's still my fault. The greatest part is that I never asked for your advice in the first place!! A boyfriend is supportive of his partner and the decision he makes, even if they blow up in his face (ya know, the whole "catch me if I fall" idea). Romantic relationships are 2 equals coming together as 1 relationship. You don't allow this dynamic to exist...and I don't like, appreciate, or benefit from your way of running the show. I AM AN ADULT. And I'm doing just fine on my own...I think that this whole father figure pattern is probably a consistency through all of your relationships, whether you see it or not it's pretty clear to me in what you've told me about Rob, Mark, A.J....And ps-it has nothing to do with you being older, it has everything to do with the dynamic you create so I hope you hear that. I have to say it is the #1 reason why I keep things from you: because I can't say "things" without you telling me your ideas and what you'd do differently. Then, if I do things my way it's clear that you are disappointed...I don't like getting set up to be met with disappointment from you. "Disappointment" is something that parents show towards children, NOT something typical in a relationship of equals. Again, I am an adult, and if I needed my dad's guidance I'd call him…

I think just about every time I have shut down, walked away, or said, "we're not talking about this right now…" the paragraph above is exactly why. I don't like feeling like I can't share things with you, but if I don't ask for your advice I probably don't want it. And I can't share a lot of things without you playing devils advocate or whatever, when all I would want was to vent…

Switching gears back to how they were in the beginning of this e-mail…If the HIV tests are your reason for assuming I was whoring around then perhaps you don't listen when I do share things with you because you were there every step of that decision…Remember when I freaked out because Nowee (sp?) topped me but not you or Chris and I was thinking "I don't even know this kid…" and I was worried he may have something? And then remember when I told you right before we got in the car to drive…somewhere?… that I was buying HIV tests on ebay but they were hella expensive…and then when I gave you the 25 I told you that you could get 100 from overseas for less $$ than you could spend on 2 tests in the US??? I kept you informed throughout that, and when I gave you that bag it was so future situations like the 1 with Nowee wouldn't arise because there'd be tests for before anything happened…it was not my way of saying "slut it up, just don't get HIV…" but if that's how you interpreted it, I hope at the very least you've been using them…

Where do I stand now? Well, I thought I'd been pretty clear letting you know that half of the times I showed up in town my motivation was primarily because I needed to get laid ASAP. I have days in Raleigh where I masturbate so many times I feel like it's becoming a problem…but I don't seek out another person, I always knew you were only 2 hours away. I think I've only been out 3 times in the 6 months I've been here, and 1 of those nights was a trivia night…I think the part that makes me feel the dumbest is that I was bringing you that book that I'd been working on. Maybe your gonorrhea scare was a head-up…or that I found that chlamydia test on your passenger seat right before I moved…forgot about that 1. god i'm a fucking idiot.

On January 6th, 2014 (1:57 p.m.), Jon wrote back:

I may be guilty of giving unsolicited advice and engaging on topics that I may or may not be knowledgeable on. If it's something I know about I may be more inclined to be unwavering in my position. If it is a topic that is new I may offer an initial opinion and listen to others positions and then weigh the entire conversation and form an opinion. I love analytical conversations and have them all the time with people. Unfortunately that's not the case with you. I'm not saying I never step over the line when dishing out my opinion however there is very little that comes out of my mouth beyond hey how's your day been and do u want to smoke a bowl that is not either shut down, dismissed, or off the list of things we can discuss. I'm sorry u think I come across as a fatherly but if u ever took the time to be more open to talking about things you would find out I'm not as dumb as u think I am.

On occasions like last Saturday night when I gave u the heads up that u were making a spectacle of yourself, you immediately thought that it was just me and that I was being paranoid when really a simple thank you and corrective behavior was probably in order you give no credence at all that what I was saying maybe true and in fact turn it around that I am paranoid. I have probably done you no service by keeping my mouth shut as often as I have about how your behavior is perceived when you're out at the club but your reaction is always the same as last Saturday I've just given up trying. The fact that it is so disrespectful to me is a whole other issue and the fact that u seem to escalate the crazy behavior when it is brought to your attention is really fucked up. The who cares defense is ridiculous. The fact that I'm the owner of the business and you're my boyfriend and that perception does matter should be enough up to have you show a little more respect. I can think of a couple of occasions where you've called me out when I was getting out-of-control and I tried to get a grip. I trusted that you wouldn't just come up to me and say this and I certainly didn't accuse you of being paranoid or that I that The Meth affected me so bad that I'm imagining things and then proceed to treat me as if I had done something offensive to you.

The absurdity of how that incident was handled is in a lot of ways typical of how you react to me. and if that is what you're calling me being fatherly then I'm guilty.

So I do not know how to come to an understanding on the communication issue because I'm sure it is off limits for discussion with you.

Before I made it through reading that entire email, I fired back (at 11:52 p.m.):

> I'm stopping half way through to say this: I walked over and asked someone who had been sitting there when we walked by if I had been calling attention to myself JUST LIKE YOU SUGGESTED I DO. The person said "no". Sooo…I did what you asked, got the answer you didn't wanna hear, and you STILL won't let that go? Seriously??
>
> it's hilarious that you can pour me G before we go out and then berate me for behaving disrespectfully towards you. what a fucking joke. g'night

On January 7th, 2014 (2:56 p.m.) Jon responded with:

> You sort of are missing the point of bringing up the incident at the club although I do not know what u think my motivation may have been to call ur attention to the fact your behavior was catching some stares. You are either naive or just trying to deflect your anger towards me but ur not stupid and when the time comes u will recognize that I was only trying to point something out that any friend would do under the same circumstances.
>
> Anyway as much as you don't care to communicate with me on issues of substance I cannot be in a relationship where I cannot communicate with my other half. I would say I would change but when it comes to the issues that create the big riffs between us I doubt I could do that anymore than i could watch u walk in front of a moving vehicle without trying to stop you. I understand the need

to Learn things on your own and believe me there are more incidents where I've kept my mouth shut than those I've provided advise or opinion.

I care about you and wish the best for u but we probably should have stayed on course to just let things fizzle out amicably.

On January 7th (10:15 p.m.), I responded with:

If you've been as miserable as it sounds like you have for as long as you have then I'm not sure why we've been together this long. I guess I didn't realize you were *that* unhappy. I would've walked away a long time ago had I known…I'm not trying to see how long I can keep u trapped in something u don't wanna be in.

Not quite sure how much you refrain from saying to me but it sounds like a lot. I feel like I only shut down what you were saying when you were trying to tell me how to run my life or giving me advice that I felt obligated to follow or face disappointment. Whatever else you kept to yourself was your choice, I know I didn't ask you to keep everything to yourself…

And as for letting things fizzle out amicably, I wasn't expecting to force you into a long distance relationship when I moved up here. It was when I asked you to please leave the dogs with me any time you were going out of town and couldn't take them with you, to which your initial response was, "Won't you be coming with me?" That gave me the impression that you weren't over it just yet…and since I got here I thought things between us were going a lot better than they apparently were. Guess I had to find I was alone in that boat sooner or later.

Jon responded (1:52 a.m.) with:

I didn't say I was miserable, and I had thought things had improved quite a bit since u move but it may just appear that way.

I have felt for a while that u were ready to go. The communication problems seem symptomatic of someone that's stuck in something they don't want to be in to me. It seems like a lot of what comes out of my mouth annoys you and I've been there so I know how it is. So when the talk of moving started I had accepted the fact that u were leaving and started to detach myself from the bf role. Was totally convinced when I left u in Raleigh the first time that we would be switching gears to friends status. After receiving the note having no agenda and like I said I wasn't miserable so I thought there is nothing wrong with playing things out and see where they go. I think we were in harmony as to where things where going prior to the move.

No matter where things end up u have an open invite to see the dogs and me for that matter whenever u want. Call first lol.

I began my next email by taking pieces of his previous emails. (3:16 a.m.) I wrote:
"there is very little that comes out of my mouth beyond hey how's you day been and do u want to smoke a bowl that that is not either shut down, dismissed, or off the list of things we can discuss."

"I'm not as dumb as u think I am"

"…so disrespectful to me…"

"Communication between us has been a problem from the beginning of our relationship"

"I have grown to accept this way of operating. It helps keep our day to day relationship uncomplicated and reduce the conflict between us however I think it comes at a cost to intimacy, passion, understanding, trust and friendship."

You don't have to say the word "miserable" for me to get the picture. These are the words of someone in a miserable relationship. And as much as you insist I shut you down at every turn I have no idea what it is you feel like you can't talk to me about. No, I don't wish to dwell on the fact that I'm on probation, nor do I want to relive the police incident any further, but other than those topics what all are you biting your lip about? If you say something and I feel differently, I'm going to let you know. Is that dismissing what you said? I'm not sure if that's what u are talking about…

Finally, thinking back on Saturday night and the embarrassment I caused you, if you remember what led up to the lecture you gave me, you and I were walking and having a lighthearted moment that turned into play-fighting (i.e., we were joking around). Then you abruptly ended the lighthearted moment to let me know that all of the people who you claim were staring may not realize I was kidding around. That's the event as I remember it. I wasn't high, just irritated by what a big deal you were making over (what I perceived as) nothing. Just to be sure we're on the same page, is that what you remember?

And 1 last thing I have to say is: In reading your account of the months leading up to my move, even though I wasn't communicating to you what I was thinking or feeling it seems you knew my thoughts and feelings exactly. So if you were that perceptive over those months, how were you completely oblivious to how I felt post-move?? I'm not sure I buy that you even thought I was "doing my own thing" here in Raleigh. You knew I was coming back home regularly and trying to get you here when it wasn't completely inconvenient for you. And without making a scene I let you know that I wasn't doing anything that could bring an STD into our relationship and that I would actually prefer it if the health department did contact me so at least I could believe you hadn't been exposed to it when I wasn't around…Plus most of my trips to see you were partially motivated by a desire to get laid. You've proven your ability to figure me out so it doesn't make sense to me that you were under the impression I was screwing around up here and that we had some unspoken agreement not to talk about it (?). I don't think u really believed that to be the case, I think u just came up with that to make yourself feel ok about your own behaviors…It never crossed my mind that I hadn't been clear enough that if u were *that* horny I would've come to town and that trolling the internet was only necessary if u wanted a DIFFERENT piece of ass…

On January 9th, 2014 (7:48 p.m.), Jon responded with:

miserable is not the word I would choose but certainly there has been better times for both of us. it has not been all bad all the time and so there have been periods where I have been hopeful that things between us would improve and periods where they seemed to in fact improve. so when you announced your intention to move without any indication that you intended on returning here or any indication that you wanted to pursue a long distance relationship i resigned myself to making the remaining time together as easy on both of us as i could. i don't know who was more ready to end the relationship but my sense was both of us around the first time you said you were moving. the business of ending a relationship is not an exact science and when all the emotions that contribute to the chemistry between two people become unstable its not unusual to go back and forth on the direction you want to take, at least that's the way it is with me.

your listing of my relationship detractors above does seem to paint a picture of a troubled union. i think the side issues you hit on are good examples of our inability to make the each other understand, respect and appreciate our rational on many of the topics we engaged. i have never intended to talk down to you, make you feel like i am trying to assume the roll of a father and im sorry that i made you feel that way. i regret my inability to appreciate where you were coming from or my inability articulate my views or suggestions on many of the issues that bred discontent.

i would give examples of conversations that were cut off or ended for other reasons by you or try to convince you that your behavior was drawing attention to yourself on Saturday and why you should care or try to further explain my belief that you were doing your own thing in Raleigh but i don't think anything i said would result in changing your views so i don't want to spend the time to do it unless you really want me to.

> i hope we can become close friends and please know i am here i whenever you need me

On January 9, 2014 (2:03 p.m.) I wrote to Jon:

> It's clear to me that u r done with us since there's no more fight in u. Your detachment from caring may actually help me to get over this quicker so thanks (?). I'll be sending a follow up after I see this client, so don't breathe that sigh of relief just yet...

The following morning on January 10, 2014 (6:32 a.m.) I followed-up and wrote:

> Jon, as much as you like to remind me that by moving to Raleigh you were completely caught off guard, you and I had a conversation about this long before it happened, and as a matter of fact we were talking about how we would navigate a long distance relationship. Do you not remember me asking you about whether or not you'd be willing to relocate? You said it would take about a year to get everything squared away as far as your businesses were concerned but that you were willing to at least consider the idea. I told you that there was no need to explore the logistics because my internship only lasted for 3 quarters so if it'd take a year to pack up I'd be done by then so it didn't make any sense...do you not remember this conversation??

Again, I followed up to my own email, continuing on January 10, 2014, (8:09 a.m.) with:

> The more I think about this the more enraged I become. I CAME TO BRING YOU YOUR BIRTHDAY PRESENT AND NOT ONLY WERE JUST TOWELING OFF FROM FUCKING SOMEONE ELSE, YOU WERE DOING SO WITH THE ONLY OTHER PERSON I'VE EVER BEEN IN A SIGNIFICANT RELATIONSHIP WITH… AND THEN LAUGHED ABOUT HOW U HAD HIS NAME WRITTEN ON YOUR WRIST…OR E-MAIL ME SAYING "next time, call first…lol"… LIKE IT'S FUNNY!?!?!
>
> I know you knew before I showed up that what you were doing in that moment would hurt me. There is no amount of speculation about whether or not I'm hooking up in Raleigh that justifies the fact that u were having a 3-some with my ex - who knows u and I are in a committed relationship - and some random dude from the internet. How gross is it that you would even try to tell me how my moving away and lack of communication somehow justifies or excuses your behavior?
>
> And ps- anyone who is having bareback sex with an internet trick and Kris McRay 2 weeks after getting a call from the health department about his exposure to gonorrhea is, by definition, a whore. I think it's laughable that somehow you can talk yourself out of that fact. It just makes me sad to think that u and I fucked 2 days before that and somehow I was dumb enough to think u were even remotely capable of being faithful… and don't retaliate to that statement, because

you knew what you were doing was wrong. You have to. Because, like you said, u aren't dumb... although sometimes I wonder if you only say you are sorry because you got caught and that any regret expressed about hurting my feelings is just a big buncha bullshit...

You know, when u send an apology email followed by a list of reasons why what you did was excusable, it totally negates the apology. I thought a brainiac like yourself would know that...

(You owe me - at the very least - to read this, think about it, and NOT fire back a response. A little more respect for a 4+ year relationship would be nice and this is just about the shittiest way I could've seen it ending...right after u meet my family no less...). You were trolling the internet for sex 2 days after I left town...REALLY!?...

I have to recognize that the real reason I'm so mad is because I'm so stupid...my delusional thinking that things between us were improving was just wishful thinking. I actually really enjoyed putting your calendar book together because it gave me an opportunity to reflect on our relationship and all that we've been through and it made me smile. Now that's all been torpedoed and I am an idiot is what it all boils down to.

That's all for now...

So, yeah, I was **mad...mad...mad...
An email exchange two days later began with Jon emailing me an address...I must have asked him for it via text? I'm speculating, because I have no idea what prompted him to send it to me as I have no record.

On Jan 12th, 2014, starting another email exchange...here's what I wrote:

Dear Jon,

Thanks for the address and for taking the time to find the answer. I appreciate it!

I wanted to write to let you know that moving forward my goal is to try and be transparent when I communicate with you so that you always know the intent behind my actions and words from here forward. There won't be any need to speculate if I'm laying it all out, and I figure if a lack of communication is our biggest issue then if I start off over-communicating then eventually I'll figure out how to strike a better balance. For now, cluing you in a lot of details along with my thoughts and intentions will set the stage for more open lines of communication. (I'm hoping anyway)

So first thing's first: I wonder if part of why I felt our relationship was headed in a better projected direction but you were less convinced was at least partially because of a lack of checking in with one another. I have thought about you or talked about you with somebody every day since I moved to Raleigh. Truthfully, some of those times were toward the end of the day when it dawned on me, "I don't think Jon and I have had any contact in 3 or 4 days..." after which I would typically just go to sleep with the intention of texting you the next day. Perhaps I was assuming too much by thinking that just because you were out of sight you would somehow know you weren't out of my mind. I'm intentionally telling you that from now on when I think of you I'll be texting shortly thereafter (and sometimes calling if I'm feeling like really switching up the game…) rather than just telling myself that whatever ran through my mind is something I'll ask you about or tell you about later (and then forgetting about whatever it was altogether…). This seems like sort of a silly thing to spell out in such great detail, but a massive influx of texting compared to what's been the norm may be unwelcome, which is why I'm warning you ahead of time. You were on my mind quite frequently for positive reasons in the last couple of months, and if I didn't let you know that then I guess I'm trying to do things differently now.

That's all…probably a lot of words to say something simple, but I want you to know where I'm coming from…

-Bruce

He responded with:

It sounds like a lot of communicating if I'm reading your email right. It's probably more than necessary I would think. More importantly would be to communicate because you want to communicate and maybe you do now. I'm still wrestling with Why you have had this major turn around about your feelings towards me. I I haven't changed in anyway that I know of and i'm not sure what has brought this on other than the reality is harder to handle than expected. I have been thru enough breakups to have experienced doubts about about getting out of the relationship that previously I felt confident I wanted to get out of. And every other time at the end of the day the break up still happens because once back together the same issues that were in play before are still there.

And he followed himself up with:

> That said this is not every other relationship and I need to look at the one I'm in now on its own. I thought maybe it would be a good idea if we both wrote down the likes and dislikes we have about each other and try to see if there is enough pros on the list that would argue for trying to rebuild something back. I use the word rebuild because that's what it feels like it would have to be for me. Like I said I pretty much thought this was over six months before you ever left. It's been those break up butterflies that have kept me from Ending things sooner myself I think. I think it would help me to do this exercise but I'll have to work on it tonight cause I have to go to hotel today. I'm suppose to leave for ac for the borgata winter open tonight but probably will put off for a few days in order to finish hotel work … Let me know what u think

And then I said:

> This isn't break up butterflies for me, this is feeling like we have something I see as worth fighting for that got buried under a pile of crap. Getting some distance and doing a great deal of thinking about whether it's worth getting out the shovel and digging through that crap, I have decided that I'm interested in doing my part in the clean-up effort. I've also done a lot of thinking about what you said the other night and how

I can't just agree to make things work and then expect them to. I also thought a lot about your statement that it seems like I resent you, and while I initially dismissed this idea I now feel like I was just trying to avoid any further conflict. I know exactly what you are referring to and can explain where it comes from. I can tell you how it influenced my behavior over the course of our relationship and why it seemed to get worse or grow as time passed. Time doesn't heal all wounds and you are right, we'll have to talk it out if we expect anything to get any better. I fleshed a lot of this out with my supervisor (which made me feel much more like a client than a counselor) and he reminded me that he and Jamie went to couples counseling 3 years into their relationship because they reached the point where they either had to get help with things or end it and walk away. They just celebrated their 19th anniversary and still use some of the communication skills they learned in counseling.

This love is good this love is bad
This love is alive back from the dead
These hands had to let it go free, and
This love came back to me
This love left a permanent mark
This love is glowing in the dark
These hands had to let it go free, and
This love came back to me
                            -**This Love**, Taylor Swift

CHAPTER 32

Babe

In speaking with my supervisor about the relationship, I mention, "I'd like to think at one point there was something great...say the great relationship is under a pile of shit, and we just need to get out our shovels!" I note that I felt stupid because he'd been hooking up with people back home; meanwhile, I had not been while living in Raleigh. I go on to say that I feel stupid for not hooking up during this time and for not even really wanting to. I note that recent visits had gone really well and that I'd been excited to see him on weekends, going on to say that I felt that since I was the one who moved, it just made sense for me to be the one who did the traveling and made more of the effort.

Noteworthy realizations include me not being able to say to him, "You did this. It was messed up. You hurt me," and getting a sincere apology that wasn't followed by a (me, speaking as Jon), "But before that, you did blah blah blah"—and then Jon goes off on all the reasons why he felt like he was in a space where he could do that because of what I was doing before that he never communicated to me—"cuz to me that's like, what's the point of apologizing if you're then going to fly off the handle about all this stuff that you've never brought up before you were being confronted? It feels really immature to me." My supervisor described this as him "salvaging his ego," noting that if he were to apologize, he would then have to accept that he hurt me and that may lead him to have to think of himself as a bad person.

On the topic of apologies, I go on to say, "He's never apologized and meant it. I talked myself into believing I didn't need him to own it. I just needed him to alter his behavior. But if he doesn't alter his behavior either, then it's like, why…I feel like an idiot when I say all this back. But I'm sure if you asked him on the phone he would have plenty of stuff to tell you about me that I'm probably not thinking of when I'm telling you all this stuff…he's probably not any worse than I am."

When my supervisor decided to play devil's advocate, he asked, "So why would you even want to be with him?" My immediate response was, "He makes me laugh! Well, a lot of it is I'm like he used to make me laugh, and maybe he could again! I still love him a lot. He's made me happier than a lot of people ever could" (tears).

My supervisor made an astute observation, leading with the disclaimer that, "All of my impression of Jon is through you. I don't think of him as a horrible person, I don't think of him as a great person. I hear some things that you're not communicating, that you're doing…but I hear that there's a real avoidance from him. So he's gonna tell you what you wanna hear but then he's not gonna put any energy behind it."

Yes! Nail on the head.

In the call with my supervisor, I retell the most recent face-to-face interaction I've had with Jon, explaining, "He came to Raleigh. He came that night [that I caught him]. I was unable to speak because I was crying so hard. He hasn't shown any feelings, like, at all…And I called him a sociopath, which I know isn't probably helpful. But I don't wanna cry anymore over something that the other person doesn't feel anything about."

Some people never cry because they have thick skin. Others never cry because the idea that crying is a weakness is so deeply ingrained in them that their walls are impenetrable in that regard. And some people are incapable of crying because they do not experience emotions like sadness or empathy in the way that most of the world does naturally. I do not know why Jon doesn't cry, to be honest, but here's an example.

Jon's brother overdosed on heroin on his property and Jon found the body. Jon and Tommy had just been in Vegas and Tommy hit the jackpot on a penny slot. He took his winnings back to our beachside town and bought the heroin that killed him. While Tommy probably wouldn't have wanted people to cry over him in the first place, Jon was likely the family member most able to respect that wish. Personally, if my brother died, I know that I would cry. But Jon and I are not the same person. (And now the penny slot "joke" makes sense. But still, especially given all the info, there is only one person I can imagine might have chuckled, and that is Jon.)

About the infidelity piece and how to heal moving forward, I tell my supervisor that in relation to Jon, "I hate playing detective. I always know *when* to play detective. I'm really in tune with him. He thinks I'm crazy. If I accuse him of something—of cheating—I pretty much know I'm right. If I think he cheated, he did. But unless he's backed into a corner and I have the evidence, he won't admit to anything. I'm like, how much effort do I wanna put into figuring it out, the who, what, when, where…?" (Because even though he'll never admit there's any truth to this statement, the sentiment, "**You're the only thing I know like the back of my hand**," is painfully accurate, especially at this time, in relation to him.)

Keep in mind that I was dating this man as I progressed and eventually completed my master's in mental health counseling. I learned more and more about human behavior and thinking while living with him, and I've always challenged his behavioral patterns. He's predictable. The problem is at this point, I'm cocky about calling him out and tricking him into saying things he'd just been denying there was any truth to. I will say things about the negative influence he has over others he's closest to, and there's so much evidence to back it up that he simply has no counterargument. Now, whether he spends any time reflecting on the things I bring to his attention, I have no idea. Whether or not he cares about any of these things, I do not know. But, when presented with the information, my only hope is that internally something will get triggered. Because I believe it matters to him what other people think of him. In a lot of ways, he is undeniably a negative influence on a lot of people, many of whom I care about to this day.

Present day, I have let go of the idea that I need him to agree with me, about anything, really, especially behavioral observations. He's made it this far, being the way that he is. The only thing that I can do is try to create something positive with what I've learned, whether I learned it through him, from him, or in spite of him.

Finally, in summarizing where Jon and I left things, as I'm speaking to my supervisor, I say, "It just makes me sad. Because if the stuff that he comes back with whenever I confront him with something, if that really is the reason that led to his derailed [cheating] behavior…or if…cuz we really started on a rough note…but if that's what screwed it up or whatever. Whatever percent of it was 'my bad' that got in the way…it makes me really sad that I didn't recognize that I was messing things up at the moment"—sobs—"and I wish I could take those back."

> **Maybe I was naive got lost in your eyes**
> **And never really had the chance**
> **My mistake I didn't know to be in love**
> **You had to fight to have the upper hand**
> **I had so many dreams about you and me**
> **Happy endings, now I know**
>   -**White Horse**, Taylor Swift

Taking responsibility is a real challenge for some people, whether it's because of an inability to self-reflect or an ego defense or a deep-seated insecurity, it doesn't matter. I just appreciate that I can make better decisions and think of other people's feelings and act according to unselfish motives as I live my life in the present day. Recognizing I can't change anyone has been helpful. I've recognized that changing Jon is impossible. And the things I know to be true about him, at least from my perspective, just *are*; whether he cares to acknowledge them or not is no longer important to me. He doesn't *have to* change a goddam thing about himself, and even better, he doesn't have to listen to me try and convince him he should want to ever again either.

CHAPTER 33

Honesty Is the Best Policy?

Here's an email from February 2014 in which I was taking this honesty thing too far:

> Hey,
>
> I feel the need to write and tell you that last night I went out, drank too much, and almost hooked up with someone (almost meaning I went in his house when I shoulda just dropped him off. I sobered up enough to realize I was being an idiot and left). I'm glad it didn't go any further than it did but I still felt like I needed to tell you because I feel guilty.
> I hope you are feeling better from being sick. I need to see your face soon!
>
> Xoxo,
> Bruce

Upon reflection, I should have fucked the guy I'm talking about and kept my happy ass in Raleigh. But more importantly and before I go screwing someone else, I should've told Jon we were done. I should've wished him well and quit trying to use my education and experience as a therapist to try and "fix" him. Jon didn't sign up to be "fixed." He knew what I was in school for, but at the same time, I recognized he didn't see the psychoanalysis onslaught that his future would inevitably hold, just by continuing to date me. LOL.

"I see your face in my mind as I drive away…cuz none of us thought it was gonna end that way"—should've happened by now. (But no worries! It's coming!)

May 22, 2014: This was (supposed to be) my last day at the university counseling center. I had gotten all of my hours under direct supervision and things were looking up, career-wise.

May 31: I officially graduated with my master's in mental health counseling.

June 6–9, 2014: We went for another One Magical Weekend experience. Also, a hella fun time. However, this year my only sighting of a porn star was when I was getting off the elevator in a wet bathing suit and I slipped and bit it (hard) on the tile floor. This porn dude from Falcon Studios, a guy from early 2000s fame, asked me if I was okay. LOL. #embarrassed.

September 4, 2014, email titled "Urgent" (2:07 a.m.): "You ballz…my mouth…NOW!!!"

At 12:31 p.m.: "You ballz. My mouth. Pronto."

I'm glad to see I was still trying to keep our sex life alive, even if in retrospect these emails that I sent are ridiculous.

I was going home frequently on the weekends with Halloween being no exception.

(I realize I told Jon I would never speak about this again as long as he promised to do the same. I guess I couldn't help myself.) :)

December 8, 2014 email titled "Hello!"

Hey Jon :)

2 things:
1) I just randomly looked at the story I posted a couple of years ago on CopBlock.org and noticed what another person had posted in

response to my account of what happened. Here's their response:

tbevin • 2 years ago

I am hearing impaired and a few blocks away from my home in 2010 with my service dog. Officer R. Ripley, badge #315, fractured my right humerous for asking if I am being arrested and, if so, the reason. It has taken almost 2 years to get the case dismissed. I, like you, was charged with resisting arrest. Ironically, the officer was already under investigation for "excessive force" at the time. He had over 10 complaints within the year of 2010. This is reason for an internal affairs investigation. This took almost 2 hers to learn; however, I knew I did nothing wrong and waited it out.

Hold your ground and peace be with you even if your attorney tries to plea bargain.

Isn't that crazy!? I wonder if it's true...ok, 2nd thing:

I just got home and emptied my pockets, only to realize...I accidentally made it home with your keys to Ibiza. I'm sorry! I'll bring 'em back to you...don't be mad!

That's all. Hope you have a great week, and don't forget...I LOVE YOU! ;)

Xoxo,
Brucey

So generally speaking, things were going well. I was genuinely looking forward to seeing Jon on the weekends and somehow we seemed to be getting it back together following the "surprise."

CHAPTER 34

Sometimes the Snow Comes Down in June

January 30, 2015—this was one of the most fun trips I ever took with Jon. For any gay man who has the funds necessary to go on an Atlantis vacation, I highly recommend it. Whether you're traveling solo or with a partner, it is a guaranteed fun time. And this trip was no exception.

Jon and I packed all of the costumes and accessories to ensure we were equipped with what we needed for the parties, and off we went. I know we stopped in San Juan, Puerto Rico along our voyage, but I couldn't tell you where else. The parties were epic. Our photos from the boat are some of the best I have from our time together. (Possibly because some of those photos were professionally done. I stole photos from the professional photo people who were trying to way overcharge for them. They'd already printed them, so if we didn't end up with them, they were just going to be discarded. That was my justification anyway.) They were so great! And the ones I took of us getting ready for the army-themed T-dance, where we are both in camo and I've got my face painted. This trip was a blast! Ten of us went, and it was more fun than adults are *supposed* to have; it's kind of like a combination of Halloween and a circuit party, every day, for a week.

Vanessa Williams performed (Jon's favorite…nah, just kidding) "Save the Best for Last" and "Paint with all the Colors of the Wind."

At that time, of recent *Desperate Housewives* fame—*that* Vanessa Williams. She was awesome.

Anyway, it was a great trip, and without all of the bullshit day-to-day stuff that sometimes tripped us up, we had a lot of fun.

On March 20, 2015, our good friends got married! I rushed into town for their nuptials and got into a minor accident…but I made it! Congrats!

Taylor Swift at the PNC Arena in Raleigh. I was there! June 9. If you don't know the term "queening out," well…that was me at the Taylor Swift concert. She was my snowflake 😊

CHAPTER 35

Karma?

I have no idea if Jon would agree that these two life events that he experienced share similarities, as I have never brought them up to him. Admittedly, I was only in his life for the more recent of the two, but I did hear first-hand accounts of the first event from him as he told me all about his work history…

The club (his club) had a handful of managers over the time I was with Jon, beginning with Kristine. Any time the club was without a manager, Jon would step in to temporarily run the show, but he didn't like doing this for long and would quickly try and find someone to fill the spot.

Later in our relationship, Jon hired a guy named Shaun to manage the bar. As far as I could tell, Jon had little to say about Shaun as a manager, which was a *majorly* positive sign when it came to Jon! As a noncompliment giver, if I wasn't hearing all the things a manager was doing wrong, it meant they were doing what many would describe as a really good job. And Shaun always appeared to be working hard and on top of things when I'd be out at the club, giving Jon little to worry about or fuss over. (This was not the norm for Jon, but I don't have time to write that book. Plus, *Bad Management* is Jon's book to write anyway.) And so the club appeared to be running as close to "on autopilot" as I'd witnessed over the years I'd been with Jon. That is, until a friend of mine from college who also knew Jon was in town from California, and while floating around on a pool raft, he casually mentioned, "Oh yeah, Shaun just became an owner [of a gay bar a few blocks over from Jon's bar]." Wait…what?

Jon had to do a little digging to see if there was any truth to this absurd claim, but sure enough, the friend was speaking the truth. Shaun was thinking he could own a bar, manage another…and from Jon's perspective, try to do both with Jon being none the wiser. And Jon was not happy about this.

Now, allow me to **pick you up and we'll go back in time** to a story I've heard countless times when Jon was the manager at the downtown Hilton Hotel. It was during his time as the manager that Jon purchased the neighboring property and became the owner of the Coral View Hotel. The folks at the Hilton may have used claims that Jon "stole" wallpaper as their official reason for terminating his employment, but according to Jon, it was because he had bought the Coral View Hotel and that's what they were really mad about.

So whether Shaun took a note from Jon's playbook or **karma** simply came back around, both the Hilton and Jon's bar lost quality managers due to remarkably comparable choices made by those managers.

CHAPTER 36

So It Goes

August 27, 2015, was Erik's celebration of life ceremony. It was held at the conference center that was part of Jon's hotel property. This was a really sad day. Erik had a really good heart.

I don't need to include "**Soon You'll Get Better**" as a suggested listen to get teary-eyed when I read that part. But if you didn't know Erik, that's the sentiment. And I don't even mean to suggest he and I were closer than we were; he just really was a great person.

On September 19, 2015, we went out on my friend Lee's boat with the dogs for a day in the sun.

On September 27, 2015, Jon and I were in Maine for his niece's wedding. That was a lot of fun! We got some cute photo booth pics while we were there (generally, we did not take a lot of pictures), and the reception was hella fun.

I turned thirty! Then Jon turned fifty-four. I liked celebrating my birthday, which we did that year in Atlanta. Jon did not like celebrating his. For his fiftieth, I was testing the waters for a potential surprise party. He made it very clear that he would be leaving town if he had even the slightest inkling that I was making moves in that department...and he wasn't kidding. So I dropped it. Fortunately, his birthday is one that everyone is naturally celebrating. (Hint: "**There's glitter on the floor after the party...girls carrying their shoes down in the lobby.**")

Speaking of that day you find yourself **cleaning up bottles** and the **memories** you **hold on to**...I was helping Jon to set up for the

New Year's Eve celebration at his nightclub. The club had put out promotional posters about the $500 balloon drop that would be happening at midnight. As we were putting cash and glitter into balloons, Jon pocketed $100 of the $500. His justification was, "Why not? No one will know...so what's the big deal?" I found this to be infuriating beyond belief not just because this was a reflection on Jon's morals but because I had been dating this man (*this asshole is what I was thinking...*) for years and years and years at this point, and he didn't get why this was problematic. Jon, who has plenty of money, was okay with shorting his patrons because they'd be none the wiser. Well, I was not. I went over to the ATM, paid the fee, got $100 out, and stuffed the remaining balloons. I don't recall how much I let on that I was irritated or if I even told him I stuffed the balloons behind his back. But at that moment, I could not believe that this was my boyfriend and that he just didn't get it. Perhaps it was **the moment I knew.**

CHAPTER 37

Run

February 28, 2016, is the date of my once-and-for-all break up with Jon. We had gone to meet friends for dinner at a restaurant in an area of town called Mayfaire, which was a pretty standard event. It was in the car on the way home that things erupted. I cannot tell you today what we were even talking about, but a realization became so evident to me as we were arguing. It was like a "**the saddest fear comes creeping in, that you never loved me, or her, or anyone, or anything**" light-bulb moment. "You just *do not* care. You *do not* care about me *at all*, and I am such an idiot because you actually never have." In that moment it felt like I'd never seen things as clearly as I was seeing them then. I wish I could say that that was as animated as I got; unfortunately, I punched Jon in the shoulder a few times as he was driving. (Lucky for me he was occupied because if he'd wanted to he could've beaten the crap out of me. He was a lot stronger. This was the first and only time anything physically aggressive had ever happened between us, but lucky for me Jon isn't an-eye-for-an-eye kind of person.) He tried to kick me out of the car that day on Market Street, but I wouldn't get out. "Just take me home and I'm gone." So that's what he did, and I was. Gone, baby, gone.

I had not planned on attending the Quest: Sober on the Beach retreat, given that I was not a member of AA and I had plans to spend my weekend with Jon, but once those plans were out the window, I left Jon's and headed to Myrtle Beach. I had friends in AA and I knew one of my closest friends would be there performing in the drag show. This was the absolute best decision, and I don't think Nick has any clue how much getting to laugh my ass off on the same day that my relationship imploded actually meant to me. Rather than ugly cry on my drive to Raleigh, I got to cry lightly as I headed to Myrtle. And then I got to see my friend, who is not an actual drag queen, give the most amazingly hilarious performance of Lana Del Ray's "Summertime Sadness." And so the day I saw Nick do drag… and broke up with Jon…made that day bearable.

On 3/11/2016 I emailed my results of the hopeless romantic test to Jon. We were in talks about whether we should try to figure things out…

In the Hopeless Romantic Test (PsychologyToday.com), my result was 71/100.

> According to your score, you are a bit of a hopeless romantic. Rose petals, poignant poetry, tall glasses of wine, touching moments, and sweet words are all loving gestures that you enjoy receiving as well as offering. Romance is fairly important to you, and likely an aspect that you consider fundamental in relationships. Keep in mind however, that problems may arise if you are with someone who really isn't the romantic type. If you look forward to Valentine's Day to express your love and your partner doesn't even acknowledge it as a special day, you might end up feeling neglected or your efforts unappreciated. Nevertheless, even if your partner isn't as romantically inclined as you are, try to be appreciative of his/her efforts when she/he does try to woo you. Some people aren't comfortable displaying their affection in screamingly obvious ways, but this doesn't mean that they don't care, they simply prefer to be more subtle.

(I recently retook this test, and I scored 76/100.)

Jon's results in the Hopeless Romantic Test were 49/100.

> According to your score, you are what we'd call a "borderline romantic." Although you're not the type who will go all out in the romance department, you do enjoy the occasional gesture of love. Romance in moderation is perfectly fine and doesn't mean that you can't experience love and relationships as deeply as your more "romantic" friends. However, problems may arise if you are with someone who is either more or less romantic than you. If you look forward to Valentine's Day to express your love and your partner doesn't even acknowledge it as a special day, you might end up feeling neglected or your efforts unappreciated. On the other hand, if your partner is more of a hopeless romantic, she/he might end up feeling a little hurt when you don't show as much enthusiasm for romance as she/he does.
>
> If too much or too little romance really is an issue for you, you may want to find a partner whom you are compatible with on this level. Keep in mind however, that this isn't a fundamental difference that must determine who you should get involved with.

On 3/13/2016 I emailed a couples therapist:

> **Name:** Bruce Langdon
> **Subject:** Potentially interested in couples counseling
> **Message:** Hello, My boyfriend of 5 or 6 years and I just broke up a couple of weeks ago.

We are both cautiously interested in working things out but know that some things need to change if that's going to be possible. We could really use some additional support that will help us communicate our needs to one another more effectively. How do you feel about working with gay couples? I live in Raleigh and he's in your town but since I don't work weekends I'm thinking we could find a time that would work with your schedule, if you are taking on new clients. Let me know if you have any thoughts. We've talked about couples counseling in the past but this is the first time it's felt like we won't get back together unless we get some help. Thank you for your time.

We never did make it to couples therapy. I had told my supervisor at the time that I needed someone to bounce a lot of things off of with Jon in the room, and then ask "am I crazy?" because a lot of the time I found myself feeling this way. (Spoiler alert: **We are never ever, ever, ever getting back together.**)

CHAPTER 38

Lover

Email from Jon (3/24/2016):

Bruce,

    I don't know that I would phrase it as "what you did wrong" because that's not how I see things. there are some things that make me question how compatible we are and no wrong can be assigned to that. i could say i wished you recognized certain things but im certain you feel the same way on certain issues. there are things that are good about us and that is where the indecision rest with me. it isn't easy to let go of 6 years with someone and contemplating that kind of trauma is not easy. here is my list of issues that im wrestling:

- i dont feel like you give me much respect. there are several areas where this comes up
    * you would rather avoid any discussions on topics that you feel like there may be differing opinion. it makes me feel like you don't attach any value my input. the real problem with this for me is it leaves

interesting subjects off the table and leaves us with overly homogenized conversations. (the dogs, how was work the weather and do want to smoke a bowl... and so on.) {sooo...**small talk, work and the weather**...*sorry, I had to*...}

* on the rare occasion i do let you know something you're doing bothers me instead of tapping the brakes you tend to push on the accelerator. you have admitted to doing this and it is just for
* as much as you pay me ridiculous compliments you can be swift with the sword as well.
* in spite of my raising the issue with you you think it is acceptable to go through my clothes, closet and office and claim anything you find. this is done without any consideration as to whether or not i have backups.

- when we are together we dont spend alot of time together. it seems like one of us is always walking out of a room when the other is walking in. thats two people that dont see each other all week. intentional or not it happens and it makes think there is a compatibility issue. if you think about it its not a new phenomenon it goes back years.
- for whatever reason you have rarely brought any new or old friends around and you dont really enjoy the company of my friends or acquaintances. this is most evidenced by your tendency to disappear when people are over.
- neither of us have the compulsion to get on the phone during the week. im glad for that

because i hate talking on the phone, but i think it would be difficult for two people deeply in love to do this no matter their distain of phone chat

- sex: i would like to have a more versatile sex life (if i have any left that is). i dont raise this issue often mostly because i know what you prefer and any deviation to try and satisfy me is taking away from what you would rather be doing. plus it can be hard to enjoy on those rare occasions it does happen because again i know what you like. there is not a lot you can do about this and i understand that. it is what it is

having said all these things it does not mean that everyday is a struggle to be with you. it is not. and i could be chugging along for a long time they we have up until the last month. the question are is it enough? is there more? how will i feel tomorrow? we definitely get along most of the time and aside from the things above i am generally happy.

life is short and making the best choices can be difficult and the outcome of those choices are not easy to predict.

so as i sit here writing i still dont know where i am or what to do. i leave it up to you.

Over,
J

Response from Bruce:

Thank you for that e-mail. I'm not sure what you are talking about with the sex part of the email...do you mean "more versatile" like you want to bottom more? Or am I taking the word "versatile" too literally? You said "there is not a lot you can do about this and I understand that. it is what it is" I'm confused because there is plenty I can do about this, so I must not be understanding what you're saying...?...

There are other parts of what you said that my initial instinct is to argue against, but maybe some of what you wrote that I thought had changed (/improved) really hadn't and I'm just kidding myself. I don't know...but I do know that I asked for a list and you gave me one, so thank you. I would like clarification on the sex paragraph though...Our sex life could've been easily altered to be more to your liking you'd just have to give me some indication of what you wish was different (?) I'll wait for you to respond so I'm clear on what you meant before I ramble on any further.

Thanks again for the email.

Response from Jon:

Yes I was referring to bottoming- when I say there is nothing you can do about it I didn't mean as much physically because I know u can do it but your preference is also very clear so I feel like those occasions occur with some exceptions more out of obligation than desire. I don't blame you for that because we like what we like

Response from Bruce (3/24/16):

Jon, we would've been having a lot more sex each weekend if I had any idea you felt that way. I thought for you to bottom it was more out of insecurity—something you suggested if you lost your hard on or if you weren't thinking you could get it up. Reading this message from you is confusing…I had absolutely no idea you felt this way, and I'm a little skeptical as to whether or not you mean it…and if you do mean it, I'm not sure how I was supposed to figure out you felt this way. This is the 1st I've heard. I feel like I always showed more enthusiasm when the possibility of me fucking you came up when compared to your enthusiasm while I was doing it (am I wrong?). I think you're assuming a lot if you think I've got a strong preference for bottoming, and you're selling yourself short if you think I didn't like fucking you…a lot.

That's all I've got for now.

If your partner of six years can't tell you this type of stuff without it being on their mind for a while and via email, it's a problem. And it isn't like talking about sex was taboo with us; this absolutely could have been a conversation we had. I just think at this point the effort and energy needed for communication was just gone, but that is my opinion as I look back over these emails all of these years later.

'Cause I, I still love you, but I can't

Bye, bye to everything I thought was on my side
Bye, bye, baby
I want you back, but it's come down to nothing
     -**Bye Bye Baby**, Taylor Swift

Jon got to air his grievances, and that's what I'd asked for. It dawned on me that I didn't like the person I was when I was with him, and I hadn't for a long time. The person he describes in his email is a shell of the person I was, going into the relationship. It's odd because they say that personality remains fairly consistent over the course of a lifetime, yet my personality had drastically shifted in the worst of ways. When I went to spend a weekend with Jon it doesn't sound like I made much effort to be in his presence. He mentions me not wanting to bring friends around him. I feel like that's been addressed, from my perspective, in previous chapters of this narrative, and he's not wrong. And I couldn't talk to him about much of anything, he's absolutely right. So why had I been fighting so hard for a relationship that clearly warped me into being someone I didn't recognize? And why did I keep giving it another chance when all signs pointed to incompatibility? And if Jon never inspired me to be a better person, why had I been doing this for six years? The short answer is all of the wrong reasons.

But I didn't have to do it anymore.

CHAPTER 39

The Aftermath

At the end of April, Jon left town to go to a concert with a friend of his. I had made it clear that I'd be available to watch the dogs anytime I could, so I was not surprised when he reached out to me to see if I would want to stay with the dogs while he was gone. And of course I did. I love those dogs!

He emailed while he was away (4/25/2016) just to let me know that he'd lost his phone and that he hoped we were having fun.

I wrote back to him with updates on the dogs, how the club had been on Friday and Saturday evenings, and to make it clear I was gone (by way of speaking about saying goodbye to the dogs and how hard that was). It was an uneventful exchange. A day later on the twenty-seventh, I wrote the following email:

> Hey, I sent this text yesterday before I remembered you may still not have a phone…
> Did you make it back to the land if puppies? Hope you had fun, just wanted to check in and see how my dog friends are doing…
> That's all…hope you made it home safely

And he responded with this:

> Hey thanks for taking care of the pups! hope you guys had a good time. yes made it back safely but exhausted. come down again soon!

We were getting along via email, and even though we hadn't seen each other, I don't think either of us wanted that to change any time soon.

I must have spent some time reflecting over the relationship and I was starting to make connections. On May 15, 2016, I sent the following email (which was ridiculously titled "Jon Little Baby Man the Cutest Man in All the Land try 'n' Catch Him if You Can!"):

> Sorry for that email subject line, but to be honest having no one to say your name to in weird and wonderful ways has been (quite possibly) the most difficult part of this entire breakup experience…
>
> Ok, so to get real…
>
> I find myself reflecting on your own admission that you are notorious for coming back to the ashes of a relationship and striking matches at it to see if there's anything left to catch fire. You painted this picture long before you and I were ever an item (I think pondering over your relationship with Mark, although I'm not totally sure if that's what you were referencing…). I'm bringing this up because I fully intend on coming to spend next weekend with you, but if you know in your heart that what we had is just ashes then PLEASE tell me that before I get there. I'll still come (I'm looking forward to spending time with you and the dogs, without expectation) and look forward to the trip no matter what. But it will help me to have some idea of how not to

leave in a sad state if I know what I'm walking into.

Sorry to send such a serious email when I know it's not your style…And if you are just trying to play things by ear, no response necessary. Just know that the burnt-down-house analogy will be on the back of my mind if I don't hear from you otherwise.

Brucifer

He responded with this:

Bruce,

You are correct about my past. I have in most cases gone for a second bite of the Apple with a dismal record of success. However as they say on the bottom of every brokerage account statement past performance is no guarantee of future results.

When I said I missed you last week I meant it. You have been a big part of my life for the past 6 years and saying with 100% certainty that I want to close the door on us getting back together is not something I want to do. My invitation for you to come down was because I genuinely would like to see you and want you to see the dogs. I wasn't considering it to be a "let's try to work this out weekend." I'm glad you brought the matter up because the potential for an awkward couple of days exists without some clarification of what we are doing. Your email leads me to believe you do want to work it out (I may be off here) I was not even aware that you had any interest in pursuing that.

> Your request is forcing me to use my brain and give you an answer to a question that I am not sure of the answer. I think the best way to treat the weekend would be to approach it like we are resolved to be friends but keep the door open for more.
> I know this note may confuse you more than help.

And I followed up with this:

> Thanks for getting back to me. I agree with the mentality you mentioned for the weekend. I am very excited to see you and Friday can't get here soon enough.
> Hope all is well!

Fortunately, we remained broken up throughout this visit.

Total tangent time

My favorite part of the day was waking up next to Jon. I was almost always the one whose eyes opened first for the day, on any given day. And I can't tell you how much time I spent watching him sleep. Listening to him snore, often in sync with Blackie, was one of the most comforting sounds to me. It was like I just knew everything was going to be okay, listening to him and Blackie breathing in tandem. Between the two dogs, Brownie was my ride-or-die bitch/best friend, and Blackie would not go anywhere or do anything unless she knew it was Jon-approved. She was his shadow. For a time, my most comfortable moment from day to day was when the four of us were snuggled up in bed together. Jon made a ramp to ensure Brownie and Blackie could get up in the bed anytime they wanted, and if either of us were in the bed…they wanted up. These little Chihuahua dog daughters of ours were spoiled beyond belief, but to this day they are one of the best parts of the relationship that I had with Jon. They have my heart.

Brownie Bruiser would army crawl across the bed and I would talk to her about how cute she was 24-7. Jon also regularly speaks to the dogs as if they are people...because that's how we roll. (Jon noted that he speaks "Dogwanese") Brownie and Blackie are sisters and both look like they have eyebrows painted onto their cute little dog faces. Brownie is chestnut brown with honey dot eyebrows and Miss Blackmore also shares this same feature. She's just black. You can tell they're related, but it's uncertain who the alpha dog really is. These dogs love us so much and we return the sentiment. They are the cutest little dogs and I love snuggling up with them.

The only problem they have...

And it's really a nonproblem...

Is that they're...

Uh...

Mean.

Sooo cute, but sooo likely to take a small child's finger(s). For as much as they love me and Jon, they are...well...let's just say..."protective." They are so cute, sweet, and cuddly with me. But to a new person or a kid...they aren't having it. They are loyal and loving to me and Jon, but to anyone else...no dice.

I love these dogs.

Blackie and Brownie liked "surfing"—riding in the car with the window down. They are definitely wind-through-their-hair-sunshine-loving dogs. But when I took them to Petco and inquired with the trainer about their temperament, I learned that socialization for dogs, or more specifically for Chihuahuas, is something that pretty much gets locked down in the first sixteen weeks. And guess how old these little ladies were, at that time? Yep, you guessed it, sixteen weeks old. So we were in Petco, and the two little kids who were inquiring, "Oh, they're sooo cute...can I pet your dogs?" almost lost their fingers. Not really...but Brownie did lunge at the kid as if to say, "How dare you think you have the right to pet me you little brat?" to the tune of "RARARARARARARARARAR!"

So it seemed I had missed my window for making Blackie and Brownie the social butterflies they were destined to be, but I was going to make sure to do things differently when it came time to set up my own goof troop.

When I adopted Layla and Pebbles, I knew from the start that I needed to be very intentional with how I brought them into this world, so to speak. Blackie and Brownie did not do well in crowds, they did not interact well with kids, they would try to take the fingers of both children and adult-aged people who tried to pet them, and they just generally didn't seem to like anyone other than me and Jon. And so I was very intentional about making sure to bring the new puppies around small children, groups, other dogs, etc. to ensure they would break free from the stereotype Chihuahuas have of being mean.

I also needed to be sure I didn't have "racist" dogs. (Dogs that bark at people of color are not cool. Obviously dogs that bark at black people aren't actually racist; they just react to things that are unfamiliar. I got Layla from a trailer park so there was work to be done! My goal was to make sure my dogs were essentially woke. They needed to be exposed to more than just their flying-solo-white-human-dad before the sixteen-week cutoff.) Lucky for me my friend Rosalyn was willing to participate. And while this is not my story to tell, Rosalyn had a traumatic experience from her past that involved a dog; and if I'm not mistaken, it was a mean Chihuahua, so Rosalyn was going to face her fear by meeting my dogs while simultaneously helping my dogs to be better-socialized beings. It was a win-win. (Plus, I just like hanging out with Rosalyn because she's smart and she doesn't put up with bullshit, especially not from white people.)

Anyway...so my dogs—well, my *new* dogs—were socialized with a lot of intention. And they absolutely love people of all shapes, sizes, ages, and colors; they're both Chihuahuas, and their love is extended to everybody...even Republicans.

Total tangent time over

About two and a half months later, on August 27, 2016, I wrote to Jon:

> So I know it's only August but it just dawned on me that you won't be there at Christmas when I'm with my family in Atlanta and I started getting sad...then I thought of you and how happy you would be thinking "I have the option of spending this Christmas with MY family, IF I want to..." (rather than obligated to be with someone else's family...) and somehow that made me less sad.
> #Just when you think you're over it... 😊

He wrote back a couple of days later:

> Yeah it can be hard at times and I don't want u to think that my lack of communication is intended to be as cold as cold as it may feel. I'm just trying to make it easier on both of us. Almost 6 years together so we share a lot of memories. I hope you are doing good. I'm staying busy despite not having the hotel although I don't know how that is possible. Hope to see you again soon. Are you still up for taking these two if I go out of town?

That last line had me hyped up! I responded about an hour later:

> YES YES YES to taking the 2 loves of my life any and every time you leave town! I wouldn't have bought a pair of Chihuahuas myself if I hadn't realized the awesomeness that they bring and I miss their faces more than you can imagine.

(PS: mine are slightly better behaved than yours, but in all fairness no one seems to understand why I love them so much, even after meeting them...).

Your communication hasn't felt cold so much as it's left me wondering if you're dead, out of the country, or in a new relationship. Glad you're alive! The other 2 are really none of my business. In retrospect I've accepted that although there are lovable things about you, there are a lot of things I came to overlook or accept that I shouldn't have. It's hard because you're one of my favorite people but because we were an item for such a long time I'm not sure what makes sense as far as how much we should be in contact. I like having you in my life while recognizing that at times just because my instinct is to text you I probably shouldn't...for the texts that come through, I apologize. I think about you often but realize I don't make you happy and the person I turned into while we were together isn't me. I don't know why but I like myself better when we're apart. That conflicts with the fact that I miss you sometimes, but I've known my whole life that I wanted to be with someone who makes me want to be a better person, and I knew for 6 years I didn't have that. That doesn't mean that I don't say your name out loud in awkward ways when I'm alone, or that I wasn't head-over-heals in love with you for a long time. I didn't realize that because I wasn't getting the love I needed I started changing, but in retrospect the reasons why we broke up in our first year were essentially the same things (in my opinion) that killed us in the end. I just didn't want to see it. But the time we were together allowed me to also

> see your greatness, of which there is plenty. It's hard to recognize 6 years later that you've been with a great person but a terrible boyfriend. I'm thinking you may feel similarly...?
>
> Anyway, if you ever have cause to come to Raleigh I hope you will...and the sooner B&B can come the better! Brownie will always be my #1 girlfriend, even if she has the hots for Adam... :)
>
> Hope all is well!

I had come to the realization that at least part of what kept me in this relationship as long as I was had more to do with the dogs than with Jon. Present day in my work as a therapist, I have clients that don't leave relationships they say they want to because of shared pets, so I totally get it. He responded the following morning with this:

> I don't think I could have said it any better. And I'm glad you are liking yourself more. I don't regret anything but I could see and that you were better than you were a better person and the relationship was bringing us both down. I hope to see you soon.

CHAPTER 40

The Man

When you're never made to feel you are right or it's made clear you're constantly doing something wrong by your partner exclusively, it made me personally not want to do anything for him anymore. Things that I came into the relationship happy to do or eager to help with I eventually just stopped doing. In some ways, this feels like such a stupid example, but in some ways it's perfect. From the start of our time cohabitating, all our laundry went in together. As far as washing and drying went, it was fifty-fifty between which of us did it. Folding, hanging, and putting away our clothes I usually did. Now, I'd venture to guess that everyone who has bleach in their laundry room has inadvertently gotten some small spot of bleach somewhere on a piece of clothing. I certainly have. But the number of times I got accused of getting bleach on clothes when I simply knew I hadn't, coupled with the condescending speech about needing to be more careful and paying better attention when doing the laundry, nearly drove me insane. He would regularly use bleach to do a variety of things at both the club and the hotel. I would use bleach with white towels at home. He also bleached things at home, in the house, the pool house, the pool deck, etc. and when doing laundry himself. My point is that given the amount of bleach he came into contact with compared to me, it actually makes me laugh at the absurdity of thinking how many times I got lectured if not berated over it. But when you can't be wrong, it couldn't have been you. "Jon, I haven't done laundry today, at all" would sometimes shorten his monologue. But eventually I quit doing it altogether. I'd still put our clothes away. I never got bitched at for how I did that. And when the next bleach speech kicked off and I informed him I was and had been on laundry strike, he stopped because it *had to* have been him. Although I'm sure he'd tell you the bleach incidents stopped too (but that would be a lie).

Laundry feels like such a dumb thing to focus this much attention on. It's funny to me now to think of a long-ago time, pre-Jon, when I somehow used to enjoy doing laundry. I did all of mine and Kris's—washing, drying, and folding—and I wanted to do it. Kris was always appreciative. It doesn't mean I got thank you cards or anything; it just means his response was somewhere between neutral and a thank you. But when something you do brings you nothing positive, it loses its enjoyment. I was essentially conditioned to hate laundry. It was so aggravating to be talked down to, but now it's just funny to think how much bleach he could be exposed to but still not register any accountability. But Jon, I'll be the bleach bandit. That is fine.

Suggested listen: "Dear John" -Taylor Swift (substitute the word "song" with "book").

CHAPTER 41

Dear Jon

While including that song may make me sound bitter, truly I am not (not suggesting you are either, Taylor!). At least not about how our relationship ultimately ended. Anyone who has read this far can see I had every opportunity to leave. Spelling out my reflective thoughts from recent days would get me into more **trouble** than it's worth, and a lot of my realizations are well expressed in the song "**Dear John**." My hope is that if anyone reads this text they will gain some tools around how to recognize people that just aren't good for you. With any hope, this awareness will help someone to be less susceptible to the influence of someone who ultimately doesn't have your best interest in mind.

On the flip side, if I was bitter, I'd probably write a list that looked something like this…

Things that were lost or given away as a result of dating Jon:

- Part of my tooth and the money it cost to try and repair this tooth with the dentist (which he never offered to pay for).
- More than $100,000 online gambling (poker) and the entire investment account this money came from (*minus the $3,500 I won in the Florida poker tournament, to be fair*).
- A best friendship.
- My "hopeless romantic" mentality.
- My sense of optimism about humanity and relationships.

- Six years of my life.
- Opportunities to settle down in a more traditional gay relationship with someone who shared my values (*when I was at my cutest* – vain, but true).
- Money and time forfeited for round one of career counseling in grad school (while in Madagascar with no Wi-Fi)
- Friendships with people back in my college town I intentionally kept out of touch with following the breakup (I just decided it was easier if I let him keep all of our friends…so the opposite of **and I'll keep up with our old friends, just to ask them how you are**. -**Last Kiss**, Taylor Swift).
- The (healthier) ideas I had about what a romantic/love relationship should and should not involve that I had before he and I dated.
- The self-respect and self-esteem I had prior to dating him. (I used to tell people I suffered from high self-esteem but that I was working on it…a long time ago).

But again, I'm not bitter…so pretend you didn't just see that list. 😊 And to keep it fair and balanced…

Things I gained by dating Jon:

- The memories from trips I otherwise would not have gone on (as outlined in previous chapters) (priceless).
- A knowledge of saltwater aquariums that I otherwise may not have as he agreed to fund the start-up of my first tank.
- A deep connection with two very adorable dogs who otherwise hate just about everybody (priceless).
- Money saved on rent during the time I lived at Jon's house (which I did the math on, and it totaled about $21,760).
- Furniture removed from the sublessor's apartment by Jon that was never reclaimed by them (although he has the nicer furniture from this fiasco…so that's probably a fifty-fifty split).

- A lot of knowledge about relationship dynamics, red flags, communication in relationships, and deal-breakers (can't put a price on knowledge).
- Enough content to write a book (which I can only hope will sell well enough to recoup some of the difference between money lost and money saved while with Jon… fingers crossed).

I wish that we could go back in time. I may lose some wisdom if I could rewind to age twenty-three, but the things I'd have back would make it worth it. I recognize that just because **I'd go back in time and change it, but I can't**, so moving forward is my only option.

I can only imagine that someone reading the book up until this point could be of the mentality that I (the author) am unable to take personal responsibility. I'm blaming Jon for a lot of this stuff. Sure, he may've taught me about online poker, how to sign up, and how to transfer money onto my account; but he certainly didn't put a gun to my head and say, "Gamble or else!" He didn't force me to stay with him. He was fairly explicit and upfront about reasons past partners had found him to be "challenging." He even gave me a lot of evidence that his past boyfriends had not had a lot of trust in him, based on stories he would tell. For example, he was talking about Mark one time (the boyfriend before Rob) and recalling an incident where apparently Mark had gotten a ladder and put it up to the pool house's back window to peer in and see what Jon was "up to"—to catch him cheating or doing drugs or whatever. Jon was telling this story at the time to highlight what a nutcase Mark was, but the underlying message is Mark didn't trust Jon when they were together. I'd seen firsthand that Rob should not have trusted Jon. And so for me to be surprised to find myself distrustful of Jon was a bit silly, if I'd been paying any attention (#hindsight). I've realized now that it isn't Jon who changes…just his partners do. And yes, that line is meant to have multiple meanings behind it, and they all apply.

My pre-Jon naive self **should've known** what I was signing up for. But as a naive person in the world, I had this idea that people older than myself were there to provide positive guidance to me and other people who were younger than they were. It didn't dawn on me that someone twice my age could be an overall negative influence. But gaining insight into the fact that people don't share the same morals and values has been a lesson I've had to learn the hard way.

I knew when I enrolled in college that my ultimate career goal was to become a therapist because I wanted to help people. But not everyone has a goal to help others. Some people are fine living life in a way that helps them almost exclusively. And it's not my job to change those people. I just also don't need to date them. I do have a problem with people living obliviously to the general consensus that they bring down the people closest to them. In a perfect world, there would be a healthy balance between living life selfishly versus selflessly. There's truth to the idea that if you don't look out for yourself, who's going to? But there also has to be some self-awareness when it comes to the influence important or powerful people have over others.

To end this chapter of my life on a positive note…

A valuable lesson that Jon taught me that aligns with this topic involves asking for raises. As little as Jon thought of my former front desk manager at his hotel, he did respect the fact that this guy asked for a raise. Jon noted that he was not someone who ever just gave out raises, even if people were working hard and going above and beyond, because to him that was the expectation of what they should be doing. From his perspective, as someone with an extensive background in management, why would raises be offered freely? It means less money for the business owner! So for this front desk manager to recognize his hard work and demand a raise was something Jon could respect.

All too often as a therapist, I have clients who go above and beyond as employees and over time may become resentful of their employer because it isn't being recognized—either with words or monetarily. For those clients who I know really do bust their asses and for those who I know play an invaluable role in their company, we talk a lot about assertiveness and how to have that conversation so they will be adequately compensated. I cannot tell you how many times this has worked to my client's benefit and their boss has been on board with raising the person's pay! It's all about speaking up for yourself and knowing your worth.

Less assertive people will simply let that hardworking attitude be overshadowed by resentment and eventually start to underperform or at least drop back to being an average employee. And that's fine for some. But self-esteem is built on the things we do that we can confidently say we are good at, so why be average if the alternative is to continue to go above and beyond while also being compensated appropriately and speaking assertively (thereby feeling "heard" and "validated" when your raise is granted)? The latter certainly sounds like the best outcome to me, and pushing my clients in this direction is part of what makes me a great therapist. So I do have Jon to thank for providing that insight many years ago and the influence it has had on how I approach career guidance with my therapy clients.

CHAPTER 42

Begin Again

It was very early in the month of September on an evening in 2017 when I met Nathan Jarron. Nathan and I met at Jon's nightclub. Since the breakup with Jon had been over a year and a half ago at this point and was ultimately best for both of us, we managed to get along well enough for me to occasionally visit him to see the dogs and stay out in the pool house for a weekend. Jon had a live-in boyfriend in the house, and they seemed happy and so I was happy for Jon.

So on this particular weekend I was visiting, I noticed a guy that I thought looked cute and who appeared to be living-it-up, having a lot of fun, much the same way I do when I'm at a club. It wasn't until later on in the night that he walked out of the second-floor bathroom, looked back at me, and said, "Hello! Damn. You're cute." And that's how it all began. I believe he was fairly drunk. I was buzzed.

Jon was having people over after the club so I invited Nathan to hang out by the pool. We chatted and flirted; why not? It seemed very **innocent** at this stage in the game. At some point, while we were chatting out by the pool, Nathan mentioned that he'd recently gotten into some trouble for some simple assault incident involving his adoptive mom, no biggie. But I could hang with a bad boy. Everyone makes mistakes, right? Good thing I had that relaxed mentality, given that he'd only recently been released from jail.

We moved things from out by the pool to inside the pool house, on the second floor where I was set to sleep that evening. It didn't take many questions for Nathan to really open up about some very personal things. The CliffsNotes version is that Nathan was raised by adoptive parents and his dad had sexually abused him when he was a child. Meanwhile, these adoptive parents had their own biological son not long after Nathan had come into their world, whom they consistently favored and whom the dad did not abuse. Nathan stated that without ever actually admitting to being aware the abuse was going on, his adoptive mom "had to have known...I just know she did."

Now, for a therapist to hear this info coming from the mouth of someone I already knew I was attracted to, my empathy for this guy's initial upbringing knew no bounds. I was devastated that this seemingly normal dude had been through so much and from such a young age without signing up for any of it. Not to mention that any red flag alert that may have sounded when he first spoke of an assault on his mom was now null and void, given this new info. She and his adoptive dad just sounded like terrible people. And I appreciated that he was so willing to open up about such personal things so quickly, just letting it all out, with no filter. Since we were already chatting it up while sitting on the upstairs bed...why not? We had sex.

Another fun fact was that even though we had met at a nightclub that wasn't where either of us resided, we both lived about two hours away and not all that far from one another! It felt like fate to learn that where we met wasn't either of our home bases and that we were both just visiting for the weekend. As such, he was staying in a nearby hotel, which I drove him back to the next morning. After dropping him off and heading back to the pool house, I realized he'd left his lighter behind. So, I had a reason to make the couple-of-minutes trek back to his hotel and see him one last time. This felt like it had the potential to be the start of something special.

> **I just wanna know you better,**
> **know you better, know you better now.**
> **I just want to know you, know you, know you**
> **'Cause all I know is we said hello**
> **And your eyes look like coming home**

BETTER MAN

**All I know is a simple name
Everything has changed**
                -Everything Has Changed,
                  Taylor Swift ft. Ed Sheeran

CHAPTER 43

The Archer

Nathan and I continued to text after going our separate ways. A few days later he insisted we go out on a date that night; he had big news and was very excited to share it and to celebrate. So we met at Sushi Blues in downtown Raleigh. He showed up dressed nicely with a ring on every one of his fingers (which I remember thinking at the time was a bit much. They were masculine, silver rings, but come on, still a bit over the top). Nathan explained over dinner that he had closed on a real estate deal and was pleased with how it had gone as it resulted in him receiving a big commission check. Good for him! I could certainly appreciate that he'd had a big win in his career! Working as a therapist I have clients who do just about everything and based on my real estate clients and how hard I'd seen them hustle, I could appreciate that this was a big deal. Plus, he was very animated about it, so I didn't need a dollar figure to recognize it had been a decent payout and he was happy to have closed the deal.

Over dinner, we got to know each other better. I was thirty-one, and he was almost exactly a year younger than me with our birthdays being a day different from each other. He told me how he'd earned his bachelor's and master's degrees in English and history, graduating with both degrees at the same time, from ECU. I had worked in a college counseling center for a few years, so I had seen students do dual degree programs before. (To me, this indicated Nathan was a very driven person, especially given that my own master's program came after a decent break from school altogether before I picked it back up again.) After Nathan graduated, he went on to explain, he'd gotten his cosmetology license and began cutting hair for a while. He shared that he was currently living with his best friend, Suzy, in a house on a lot of land not too far outside Raleigh in Johnston County. Suzy had been the salon owner when he initially went to work in the salon years ago. Nathan explained that he eventually got bored with cutting hair, so he went and got his real estate license, which he'd had for the past few years at this point. He'd built up a pretty decent business and had nine employees working for him out of a real estate office somewhere in downtown Raleigh. I shared with him my career path to becoming a therapist and opened up about my family and friends, what I liked to do for fun, and my dogs. It was a pretty typical first-date conversation when two people were obviously vibing.

Through back-and-forth texting, calling, Facebook messages, and face-to-face conversation, I knew that there was a lot about the dynamics between Nathan and me that had been missing in the relationship with Jon. For one, Nathan was monogamy-wired, and let it be known, that was a nonnegotiable; he was too jealous of a person, he admitted, to even try to navigate anything different. And I was happy with that.

Nathan was raised in Johnston County, which had and still has a reputation for being a bit country and a bit rough, let's just say, while at the same time having plenty of very nice homes on multiple acres. I can't tell you how many times someone has said or done something mildly rowdy or borderline offensive and then said, "Well, you know that's the Johnston County in me coming out." And Nathan was no different in that regard. More affectionately called JoCo, Nathan regularly referenced his home county as the reason why phrases like, "Well, you know me, I'm likely to cut a bitch," regularly came out of his mouth. There is very much a well-that's-just-how-we-get-down-in-JoCo attitude, both with people currently living there as well as those who have moved away to neighboring towns and counties. And so while what came out of Nathan's mouth was a far cry from the proper way of speaking I'd become accustomed to having grown up with a mother who had been an English major, typed messages from him passed my subconscious grammar screenings.

The second message Nathan ever sent me on Facebook was an article titled "One Day You're Gonna Meet Someone Who Feels Like Home." The day before he'd sent a jiggling babies video that I had not responded to. He was super sweet when we were around each other, which was as much of the time as we could be. He'd typically come to my apartment, traveling in from Suzy's to spend time there with me. We cooked eggplant parmesan together that was really good in those early days. I'd been a vegetarian since I was seventeen, and although he was not, he was totally on board with making this veggie meal.

As he spent time at my place, I began getting more tidbits related to his complicated relationship with his adoptive parents, who he referred to by their first names. I didn't want to pry, but I also didn't understand some of the ways Nathan went about the relationship he had with Barb, his adoptive mom. Nathan would come into my apartment and blurt out, "Well, Barb's being a cunt again," and then take a phone call from her in front of me where he was being sweet as can be with seemingly nothing amiss between them. He'd recall memories from childhood, explaining that when Barb would leave to go grocery shopping, he'd "throw a fit" because he didn't want to be left home with David, his adoptive dad. And there were times when he'd just rant about how much he hated Barb for this reason or that reason, both things past and present. I just remember feeling so much empathy for Nathan while also recognizing that it was hard to engage in these conversations because I'd realized that when I would engage Nathan would emotionally unravel very quickly and didn't seem to have the tools to get himself out of bad emotional spaces. So while the therapist in me wanted to help, helping Nathan looked vastly different than helping a therapy client and vastly different than how I'd help any other friend. Using the example above, if Nathan came in and said, "Barb's being a cunt again," the best response I could give would be, "That sucks," and then change the topic as if disinterested. Even typing it out now I know how cold it sounds, but if I inquired, "Oh yeah? What's she doing now?" he would start talking and talking, getting more and more angry all the way until I'd have to be like, "Are you mad at me? Because you're shouting at me…but I think you're mad at her…or mad at the situation?" And that would either be met with, "Oh, now you're trying to be *my therapist?*" or "No, I'm not mad at you…I'm just mad!" So the, "Oh, that sucks," response was just the safest alternative. Nathan had not yelled at me because he was actually mad at me, but it was becoming increasingly evident that there was a rage inside of him that I'd be wise to navigate with heightened awareness. And it wasn't all parent-focused. Often when talking about his friends who I was yet to meet would be, "Guess what that son of a bitch, worthless dipshit of a husband did to my girl Tiffany??" Now, these types of conversations it could be argued were just Nathan 'speaking JoCo' more than actually getting angry, but it was always a slippery slope. Occasionally I would inquire, "Wait, but last week you were hanging out with Tiffany's husband every day like y'all were best friends…?" Most of his relationships, I came to learn, were either best friends or sworn enemies; and just about anyone from either list could change which list they were on in the blink of an eye. I was glad to be on the good list.

I did some beating around the bush in conversations with Nathan, mentioning emotion regulation strategies I was finding to be effective with therapy clients, or going on and on about the benefits of this really nifty therapy approach called dialectical behavioral therapy. But with my passive approach getting nowhere, one day I just asked point-blank, "Nathan, have you ever heard of borderline personality disorder?" He responded, "Oh yeah, I have that. I was diagnosed with that…and bipolar…and I think anxiety, depression." Well, I was at least glad to know my diagnostic skills were intact. And that this a-ha moment didn't create any issues between us.

As I mentioned, Nathan really hadn't directed any anger at me. And he could be really, really sweet! There was one thing that I really need to recognize as a major red flag and a deal-breaker: This man *did not* like Taylor Swift. And he loved country music. So what do you do when met with such ignorance? Well, you help the person to see the error of their ways, of course.

CHAPTER 44

Forced Taylor Swift Time

Nathan had sent me a quote via FB messenger (10/2/2017) about the type of love he is looking for, how it doesn't cause anxiety, it feels like home, it's free-flowing and simple, and it's something that "allows me to be me without question." This was the very beginning of our relationship and so this was merely informational at the time.

I responded with, "My biggest fear is letting someone in enough to where this song makes me think of them, someday." Attached was the "**Last Kiss**" lyric video.

He wrote back, "Being scared of losing them?"

I responded, "Nah, I just wanted to make you listen to a Taylor Swift song. 😉"

He shot back, "You're an ass!"

I responded, "Hey, it's a great song."

His response (and here's what BPD looks like in action? "[Rolley-eye face] I already told you I've been emotional and all up in my feelings today, and you send me a song like that, and I'm thinking you're trying to be sweet and actually start to open up a little bit, and then you gonna go and say some shit like that."

I replied, "Maybe shit just got too real" (I thought we were playing fighting at most.)

Nathan replied, "Maybe you need to stop trying to fight too real…it's not a bad thing. 'Cause right now I'm scared shitless. I want nothing more than to do what's comfortable and push you away and run. However, I also want you more than anything. So stop being scared of 'too real' 'cause, baby, I am too."

(At this point we've been seeing each other for two weeks.)

I responded with, "Perhaps this will better convey how I feel about you…" (insert **Taylor Swift's "Sparks Fly"** music video with a quote written beneath, "**I'm captivated by you baby, like a fireworks show**]."

He inquired, "Is that really how you feel?"

I, being a bit of a smartass, responded, "A lot of it, yeah. Including, '**My mind forgets to remind me that you're a bad idea**,' followed by, 'But you don't have green eyes, so clearly there are some discrepancies.' 😊"

To which he said, "Ummm, my eyes couldn't be more green if you colored them with Crayola." Whoops! We were so early in the relationship that I didn't know the color of his eyes!

A week later on October 9, Nathan inquired, "Can we get married here? This place is beautiful!" and sent a link. I totally get that people joke about stuff like that prematurely sometimes in a relationship, but it felt worth noting.

CHAPTER 45

Mugshots

Now, very early in the relationship I had googled Nathan Jarron's name just to see what came up. I'm sure I also looked up his North Carolina arrest record since he'd recently been in jail, but what really mattered to me was what would be immediately googleable. Because you can't introduce your boyfriend to your parents with his first and last name if Google kicks back mugshots…you can't bring him to a work party with your colleagues in mental health if he's regularly getting arrested…and as a therapist, you must keep your boyfriend a secret when he's a known felon. And who wants a boyfriend that they can't bring anywhere, show off, or even admit to having?

(Note: It is not lost on me that there are some vague parallels between this situation and my harping on Kris over his teeth. By comparison, any dental work for the benefit of first impressions feels sooo dumb compared to this. #hindsight.)

Along with his collection of mugshots that came up in the image section, his Keller Williams Real Estate Agent pics and website were right there too. So professionally, I had to wonder how many real estate clients were okay with working with the agent that clearly had a criminal history as well. And what was even more baffling about this whole situation to me was that Nathan didn't seem to have ever considered the impression he was making on people who met him for a listing, maybe needed his contact info, Google-searched him and found, oh, he's been arrested numerous times…and recently. I mean, I'll admit, there are times when I can think up a worst-case-possible scenario and it will not pan out that way; but in this case, it seemed like a no-brainer. Anyone trying to get connected with a real estate agent is not going to pick the one with the most mugshots, especially if they're meeting at a vacant residence to look at a property.

I knew there were services that would take mugshots down or if you complained to the right person they'd be taken down. But again, it felt like inaction, and the more Nathan ramped up with things like marriage talk and happily ever after or parenting podcasts he listened to so he could be a good dad one day, the more I was envisioning a wedding at which I'd be explaining, "Yes, yes, I know about his arrest record," to any guest who had a phone. Keep in mind also that I was under the impression that he was a few weeks out from getting a big check following the closing of a real estate deal.

And so while we were having a happy time together, generally, I had made the point that, "Hey, if you ever think you're meeting my parents, you have to take care of this first," or, "Hey, our wedding day isn't going to be ruined by people bombarding me with your mugshots." It wasn't a point I brought up regularly because I was trusting if having a future together mattered to him he'd get it taken care of.

I had planned a trip to go Atlanta Pride in 2017 with some friends, and since Nathan and I were now dating, I figured bringing him along made sense. This would be an opportunity for Nathan to spend some time around some of my friends from North Carolina who would also be traveling to Atlanta and for us to have a good time in my home city. (While my parents and siblings do live in Atlanta, it would not be the first time I'd traveled home and not necessarily seen them, especially if I was with friends and it was for an event like Pride.) The dates for Pride this year were October 14 and 15. Nathan and I would be driving down together; and we'd be staying in a hotel room with a few of my friends, including Lee, who was more of a best friend, and another couple. Lee and Nathan had met one time prior, so Nathan was aware that we were close. Nathan also knew that Lee would stay at my apartment when he'd come into town to Raleigh.

The car ride from Raleigh to Atlanta was six or seven hours, so there was plenty of time to talk. Nathan finally gave me the full break-down of his family and upbringing and everything. He opened up about his biological parents, who he hadn't known for a big chunk of his life. He explained that his biological mother had a best friend who had died. The best friend came from wealthy parents who were understandably heartbroken over the death of their daughter. So his biological mom, realizing Nathan would have a better life with her deceased best friend's wealthy parents, gave Nathan to them. She never told the biological father she was pregnant; and since bio dad was in the army, deployed, and Nathan was the product of a one-night stand, this was an easy secret for her to keep.

Based on what Nathan shared, this wealthy couple turned out to be evil, telling Nathan his biological mom was a drug addict and a sex worker who had died. On top of that, his adoptive mom looked the other way intentionally as Dad sexually abused him. Nathan explained all of this to me from the passenger seat as I drove us to Atlanta. ("**And in this passenger seat, you put your eyes on me, absent-mindedly making me want you**"—nah, not quite.)

While in Atlanta, Nathan displayed overtly jealous/possessive behavior when I interacted with friends and was incredibly uncomfortable when we were meeting new people. While I would never pick on someone for social anxiety struggles, this was *not* Nathan's typical behavior. He was extremely extroverted in all social settings we'd been in up to this point. It was odd…

A few days into Pride, Nathan, myself, and two friends were headed somewhere in an Uber. I was seated up front but heard Nathan telling my best friend Lee that his biological father lives in Florida and owns a boat that between gas and crew costs about $75,000 just to take out of the harbor! (My naive self just thought, "Damn, having a boat is costly.") Lee's ears perked up. Having formerly owned a boat shop, Lee suddenly became the quizmaster, wanting to know all of the details he could gather about this fascinating boat…

When we exited the Uber, Lee rushed over to me and—speaking out of the side of his face—noted in his super Southern accent: "I don't give a goddamn if Nathan's dad owns a fucking cruise ship. There is no boat out there that costs seventy-five Gs just to take out for a booze cruise."

This is where things began to unravel.

If Nathan could lie so effortlessly about his dad's boat, I wondered, are there other things he could be lying about? (Spoiler alert: *everything*.)

CHAPTER 46

There's Nothing You Can Say to Make This Right Again

When you realize that every word that someone has fed you is a lie that you've believed for more than a month and the more you dig into details, the more discredited the information becomes, it is a terrible feeling. Here is the original list I made when I first started to believe I'd been duped titled "Things Nathan May Be Lying About…?":

- Money—bank account, "savings and trust," money made when closing the last real estate deal before our first date. Where'd all the money go? Did it ever exist?
- Sketchy behavior. Calling Cathy to try and sell a sofa for $50 because he needed it to pay his probation officer or he'd go to jail for twenty days.
- Stated he had a real estate office with nine employees when we first started dating. Described where in town it was located also.
- Reports his cosmetology license has expired. Others insist he never had one because he dropped out of cosmetology school.

- Says he's been to therapy three times...others say just one. At least one of these times he would've been late based on when he left my place, although he may've gone.
- Nathan's text: "OMG, baby! I finally got busted newspaper to give me a response. I have been trying to get up with them since the beginning." Based on screenshots their response was to his email sent *that same day*?
- "I will send you the confirmation of the receipt this afternoon after I make the payment." (Receipt never sent, lack of follow-through, mugshots still posted.) EraseMugshots.com said mugshots would be down in five to seven days. Ten days later they were not, even though N said his friend was taking care of it (again, no follow-through).
- Said he'd sent pics of bank statements confirming the savings account where he reports he deposits almost all of his money (never sent).
- Reported he'd already told his probation officer he was going to visit his dad in Florida. Later it slipped that he hadn't told her *anything* about any trip. Nathan insisted he said initially he was *planning* to tell Florida story and not that he *already* had, as he initially reported.
- Nathan said he pays *all* of Suzy's bills. Suzy says this is completely false.
- Third-party reports Nathan only just started alleging dad's sexual abuse in the last six to eight months *after* he met a guy who told him he'd made a lot of money by suing his own dad for sexual abuse. A third party also reports Nathan's dad has said he'd be "100 percent willing to take a polygraph to prove these allegations are false!"
- Nathan claims he told his therapist at their first session about his father's abuse and that the therapist agreed to get in touch with his *five* former therapists to gather their notes about his previously reported abuse allegations. Nathan previously stated his brother, the biological son of Barb and David, was not sexually abused but that he (Nathan) was. When I relayed to Nathan that I felt like I personally

needed to file a CPS report because Nathan's bro has a one-year-old son that David regularly babysits, Nathan assured me that his therapist was already going to do that. (This was after Nathan's first session.) After I warned Nathan of my worries for his well-being (given that David was about to be visited by a CPS worker armed with Nathan's report), Nathan seemed unconcerned. After Nathan's second session, I repeated my concerns, at which time Nathan stated his therapist was not going to report to CPS until after Nathan was off of probation to ensure he, Nathan, would have a stronger case. *No therapist would respond this way, given that the whole point is protecting the one-year-old, not looking out for Nathan's interest!* I knew Nathan was lying at the time, but for whatever reason, I let it go.

Since that first list was rather discombobulated, I realized I needed to get down the exact questions I needed answered to gauge a sense of what was going on, what was real, and what had simply been outright lies. Even his closest friends were telling me that Nathan was not being honest about various things that I had simply assumed to be because they weren't all that unbelievable. Here is that list of questions:

Things I need to know the truth about from Nathan include the following:

- What do you *actually* do for a living?
    - Are you yourself a licensed real estate agent?
    - Are you Pam's assistant but not actually licensed?
    - Do you own a real estate firm and actually have employees?
    - Or do you do random freelance/assistantship work for people who are in real estate?
    - Are you on disability?
    - Do you receive an unemployment (or disability) check from the government?

- Is there anything else I should know about your employment status, where you work, who you work for/with, or what you do for a living not covered in these questions that is pertinent to getting to know the *real* Nathan?
- Did your adoptive father sexually abuse you?
- How far did you *actually* go in school? What degrees, diplomas, licenses, and certificates have you earned (expired and valid) and which have you not?
- Is there anything about your parental record that you've shared with me that is untrue or exaggerated? Or anything about your life story that you shared with me that isn't 100 percent accurate? (Bio dad in Florida, met mom at a tanning salon for the first time, the Jarrons raised you without telling you who your real parents were, etc.)
- Anything else you know you need to get honest about or any questions I did not ask, now is your chance to be real with me and clear your conscience.

And finally, as I spoke with Nathan over the phone, here are the answers I got now that he'd been backed into a corner:

- What do you *actually* do for a living? **Design.**
  - Are you yourself a licensed real estate agent? **Licensed RE agent, inactive status.**
  - Are you Pam's assistant but not actually licensed? **No.**
  - Do you own a real estate firm and actually have employees? **No.**
  - Or do you do random freelance/assistantship work for people who are in real estate? **No.**
  - Are you on disability? **Yes.**
  - Do you receive an unemployment (or disability) check from the government? **Unemployment, no.**
- Did your adoptive father sexually abuse you? **Yes.**
- How far did you *actually* go in school? What degrees, diplomas, licenses, and certificates have you earned (expired and

valid) and which have you not? **BA from ECU in English and history**.

⌀Master's degree. ⌀Cosmetology certification.

I later learned that although he stated during this call that he did in fact have two bachelor's degrees, that also was a lie, or at the very least could not be substantiated. A friend who worked with him in real estate stated that he had one or two properties he closed on as a licensed real estate agent before they suspended his license. He was on disability for his diagnosis of bipolar disorder according to Nathan. I also learned from Suzy, whom he lived with, that on days when he would tell me he was running around town either showing properties or doing other productive things, he had really just gone back to her home to go to sleep.

The following I cannot make a final judgment call on because I was not there and I do not know, officially. I would never deny someone their sexual trauma. However, according to his self-proclaimed "best friend," Suzy reported to me the following.

Nathan's story about his adoptive dad sexually abusing him? That was something he heard a patient at the psych hospital share in group therapy when Nathan was there as a patient himself. Nathan's parents had him hospitalized for threatening to physically harm them and they had (according to Suzy) cut him off financially. The other patient, the *actual* sexual abuse survivor, was apparently involved in a lawsuit against his abuser and anticipated a cash settlement. Having come from a wealthy, well-to-do family who had a big name in the community, Nathan came out of the hospital with a story to tell. Nathan threatened to share his story of abuse around town unless he got what he wanted from his wealthy parents (again, according to Suzy). As far as I know, they never caved. All of this happened in months, maybe years, prior to my first encounter with Nathan.

By the time Nathan told me about his abusive childhood, I'm not convinced he didn't believe it himself.

When I realized the mountain of lies I had just assumed to be true in our short time together I felt so incredibly stupid. As Nathan once whaled at me, "Do you *really* think I would lie about something like that?" Umm...yes.

I would *never* deny anyone's report of abuse. In fact, I felt genuine hatred toward Nathan's adoptive parents and immense empathy for all that he had been through as a kid. From the first night we met up until I realized that some people can literally lie effortlessly about *anything*, I actually had feelings—romantic, empathetic, caring—for this dude. Imagine my confusion when a couple of weeks before it all ended, he informed me, "I told Barb [his adoptive mom] about you, and she can't wait to meet you! She wants to know when we can do lunch." This dude had seethed with anger as he explained just weeks earlier that "she *had* to know what he was doing to me...she *had* to!" I do not know in what world of delusion Nathan thought I wanted to meet the person who looked the other way throughout his childhood of sexual abuse (from very young until age fourteen, according to Nathan) or that I would be happy to know that she couldn't wait to meet me.

Present day, I have heard from two of Nathan's level-headed, very close friends that Barb is actually a very kind person and that she is as sweet as can be. I don't know anything about her husband other than what Nathan has told me about being abused by him. And neither of these friends who had such glowing things to say about Barb provided any insight into what David is like. While I cannot make any sweeping definitive statements about what is and isn't true from Nathan's childhood, I can say without a doubt that Nathan has lied to me about a mountain of things as an adult-aged person that, from my perspective, there was no reason to lie about at all.

I wasn't the only person he'd ever lied to, of course. He tricked the owner of the salon (Suzy, who he later lived with) into believing he had a cosmetology license and was allowed to dye, cut, and style hair for at least a couple of months. The salon owner initially said Nathan just needed to be sure and get a copy of his license to her as soon as it came in the mail (since he'd "lost" it). Eventually she figured out he didn't have a cosmetology license, which I'm guessing is when he moved out of the small town he'd been living in and realized his dreams of being a real estate agent. Scheming was just how this dude operated, I was coming to learn.

I was infuriated, confused, and ultimately felt like I was completely done with him, forever. But of course, I was not. He continued to resurface in my life for the next couple of years, and although I never called him my boyfriend again I was fascinated by him now that I knew he was full of shit. I had different lenses on now, and I could see his bullshit as he said it, and I could watch as he did and said manipulative things and I could predict what his end goal was with the calculated moves he made. We never got along again as well as we did at the beginning of the relationship. He had told all of his friends how great I was and how we were going to have a future together, only to be lying to me the entire time about who he was and what he did. And the silly thing is that I didn't give a fuck about his degrees, how many employees he had, or his pretend licenses and certificates. But I do care about honesty when it comes to a long-term partner. So at best, if I ever let Nathan anywhere near my world again, it will be as a case study to take further notes on and hypothesize about human behavior and how it is impacted by adoption trauma or something useful will have to come of it. Because otherwise I just know he's toxic and untrustworthy in a way that is mind-blowing.

And if you asked me if I miss him from time to time, **I'd lie**. He is an absolute love-bombing miracle when you're in that phase with him. And I do have to give him credit for something he did that was really sweet. He had a book created that he intended to give me on Valentine's Day. I do not know how he got it done, but it's a very sweet gift. It's essentially **the story of us**, even though we weren't together for very long, in a kid's-book format. He and I are both in it, our names as well as two dudes drawn that look just like us. And in this story of us, **we were happy**. So I am glad that in the pages of the book he gave me, Nathan and I will forever remain happily ever after. If he hadn't lied to me about—well…everything—who knows? Maybe we would've lived happily ever after. Oh yeah, the best part? The name of the book? **End Game**. He definitely got me… for a minute in time.

CHAPTER 47

I Never Trust a Narcissist, but They Love Me

And now, putting my background in psychology to good use, here's the psychological profile I typed up about Nathan in January of 2023:

> Nathan T. Jarron
> Psychological Profile
>
> Nathan T. Jarron is a 36 year old Caucasian male. Nathan is approximately 5'7" and weighs between 135 and 145 lbs. Nathan identifies as gay. Subject presents with extensive history of unstable relationships, with a tendency to fluctuate between idealization and devaluation of the people with whom he interacts. Nathan displays traits of malignant narcissism and toxic narcissism. Nathan has been diagnosed with various anxiety and depressive disorders, bipolar disorder, and borderline personality disorder. He presents as superficially charming, initially. Nathan has a tendency to be extremely irritable, which he can only mask for so long before the people around him experience his mood instability first

hand. Nathan struggles with being honest, often leaving people confused over what is real about him verses what is the reality he has created. It is uncertain if Nathan knows he is being deceptive in some instances, as certain unverified traumas reported by Nathan cannot be fact-checked. Some of these have become ingrained in his personality, as Nathan speaks words and with a tone that are highly victim-oriented. Nathan is highly antagonistic with people he interacts with most frequently. Nathan intentionally garners a sense of pity from people, often following up introductions with historical trauma he has experienced or information about people who have wronged him. Nathan has a lot of needs that he expects others to meet for him. Despite being an able-bodied and relatively young man, Nathan has not been employed for many years. He has become increasingly comfortable asking, and at times demanding, assistance from his adoptive parents or his friends. Nathan's toxic narcissism is evident when he becomes enraged by someone not meeting his expectations for a handout. Nathan appears to target people who are overly empathetic, both those who have known him his whole life as well as newly acquired contacts. One would be holding their breath indefinitely if waiting to hear Nathan say commonly used, courteous phrases, such as "thank you" or "I'm sorry." When confronted with behavior that is clearly unacceptable, there is a high probability that Nathan will tell the person why it is someone else's fault that he behaved the way that he did, OR it is the confronter's fault for having the audacity to hold him accountable. He may lie in this situation, insisting "no I didn't…" (even if he absolutely did). And whatever the behavior may be, he will not feel remorse for it. (Or, if he does, he wouldn't ever actually admit to feeling remorseful, unless to do so would somehow serve him.) While he either cannot or he chooses not to put himself in the shoes of others, he does feel compassion and empathy for 1 person: himself. He has not expressed regret for any of his own behavior over the 6 years this narrator has been observing him, as regret and shame are emotions that someone would only feel if they had 2 things that Nathan does not appear to possess: self-awareness and a conscience. This author has been fascinated by the subject for so long because my background in psychology and my personal perspective of the world leaves me bewildered by this man. How does someone become *like this?* Is it nature or is it nurture? And are there other people *like this* out there? Because this author has only met 1 Nathan T. Jarron in my lifetime, and he truly shines as a unique, purple plaid unicorn-dragon.

Let me paint you a picture [the following HAS NOT happened, it is purely speculative]:

Nathan has, as far as I know, only been violent in non-life-threatening ways toward other people, up until this point. *However*, here is a scenario and how I believe he would respond if it were to come to be a reality…

Picture it: Nathan is driving on an icy stretch of road. He gets distracted when his phone falls under the seat. He ends up digging under his seat—he was on a call, that to him was VERY important—and this resulted in a head-on collision with a family of 4. They all died, Nathan did not (again, this is hypothetical…).

Nathan would be unemotional in regards to the people he killed, unless showing tears or emotion garnered sympathy from someone he was crying in front of. A "shit happens" attitude would likely be his mentality. As for the loved ones of that family of 4? Any news coverage of them, Nathan would hate because their upset energy toward him would be burdensome. He would probably get mad at anyone who dared have the news on in his presence when these people were expressing how they felt about the tragedy. He would insist that *he* was somehow *the real victim*, and that they're somehow better off. He would feel like the fact that anybody who didn't immediately move on from this incident was his enemy, and that they should just let it go, leave it in the past, and…quite frankly…fuck off. Nathan would blame gravity for the phone falling under the seat, he'd blame the car manufacturer for not designing seats that allowed for easy access to fallen phones, and he'd blame the dead driver in the family for not driving more defensively (and for getting them all killed). Nathan would likely blurt out the statement, "OF COURSE *this* happened TO ME…EVERYTHING ALWAYS HAPPENS TO ME!." If you are reading this, let me assure you: he would say it, he'd mean it, and he'd stand by it… I have never met anyone whose brain works like Nathan's does.

Furthermore, let me say: Nathan is not a psychopath. He does not want to kill people. I would argue that he is the 'non-clinical' definition of a sociopath. What I mean is, he is devoid of empathy…it just doesn't compute. If you did something to hurt him, he would absolutely belabor the point of how deeply wounded he was and inflict guilt exponentially upon you. However, if he did the same thing to you, he'd respond with something along the lines of, "well…get over it or don't. Doesn't matter much to me…" and not give it a second thought. Or he may talk trash about you to people because you "tried to make ME feel bad!" But that's just Nathan…

At this point I'm going to send what I've written to Nathan himself, via text or email. Perhaps if he's willing to explain how he came to be this way or why he is the way he is (in great detail), there may be enough here to write a book (?). In all likelihood, if you're reading this and it's published, whatever name I'm putting for the subject himself will have been changed. Unless, of course, Nathan's inner narcissist figures this is his shot at fame. Because if you're not going to be famous, infamous isn't the worst thing…right?

++++++++++++++++++++++++++++++
End of Psych Profile
++++++++++++++++++++++++++++++

What I hate Nathan the most for, if I'm being honest, is for making me a detective. I do not want to be a detective in a romantic relationship. I just like handing someone my heart and disconnecting my brain and **flying through the freefall** blindly. I got my biggest dose of that feeling from Kris, by far, but I did get a taste of that same feeling in the early days with Nathan. Who knows if I'll ever experience that feeling again? I'd like to think I will.

But where is he?

AFTERWARD

My present-day, psychology minded self says...thinking from the perspective of another, practicing empathy, paying attention to behavior patterns and theorizing about predictive behavior, diagnosing my friends – covertly – with mental health disorders, listening to someone's backstory and lightbulbs going off as to why they are the way they are...these are just some of the fun activities that come along with being a psychologically-minded professional. But something about detailing a time when I didn't naturally overanalyze human behavior and immersing myself in the voice and headspace of a younger me has been oddly refreshing.

As I wrote this narrative, I tried to rewind my brain and remember these things from my perspective at the time they happened, recalling how I felt at that time. Also, from a developmental perspective, my brain didn't have the capacity for all the 'extra' it creates today as I went through it. I found it amusing to recognize that there's a distinct difference in my analysis of both myself and others at the time these events occurred in comparison to how I view them today. Being a therapist has given me an almost automatic tendency to try and be in someone else's shoes, so I had to temporarily suspend working with clients to be able to effectively get back securely into my own shoes and press "rewind" on my brain.

As humans, we learn from our mistakes as we move forward in life, hopefully. In less fortunate circumstances, people get stuck. I live by the belief that a mistake is only a mistake if I don't learn anything from it.

I took time away from work to write all of this out in detail and it has been incredibly helpful toward me becoming "unstuck", myself. I couldn't give my clients my full focus the way that I typically did when I had all of this swirling **'round in my head**. With any luck, someone out there will benefit from reading my story, in one way or another. My goal in writing this was not to paint anyone as the bad guy or make myself look some-kind-of-way, it was simply to tell a story and illustrate the struggles I've had in relationships while also highlighting the fun times and the unforgettable memories.

I typed this all up because I needed to unburden myself of all of the stuff that's been bogging me down and that had kept me out of touch with that happy, hopeless romantic, excited-about-life person that was so present at the beginning of this story.

Hopefully something meaningful can come out of my mistakes. If these words could help someone, somehow, it would all be worth it. I certainly helped myself by getting these words out of my head and down on paper.

I realize that to forever blame an ex for the things that were lost in a relationship rather than looking to the future and moving forward, well, at some point that just gets really old. I can't let that be how my story ends. In an effort **to be my old self again**...while carrying with me the things that I've learned...I had to make something creative out of what would otherwise just be **sad...beautiful... tragic.**

I am stuck on how to spell out this next part without sounding like I'm pointing the finger of blame. But it needs to be said, otherwise it just feels like unfinished business, based on what's been written thus far...and that is this: When I began dating Jon, he was already a daily meth user and had been for years. I became one too – because there was unlimited access, given that he had the funds and the connections to essentially never run out of the drug (**like...ever.**). I wouldn't spell that out for any other reason, except that it is important to the story. I have made the statement that Jon getting the dogs probably kept me in the relationship for two extra years (because I love them so much)...If I'm being honest with myself, I have no doubt that meth also played a role in me not leaving for so long, especially given how turbulent things tended to be at times. There's no way to quantify how much time any single variable may've kept me in that relationship, but as someone who had a pretty well-demonstrated ability to end a relationship in my early adulthood, and who knew the relationship with Jon wasn't meeting my expectations very early on…before there were dogs…I'd have to imagine meth was a major factor in keeping me there.

There's plenty more that I could say here, but it's just not my story to tell. I do wonder if there are others who can relate to my story…

My hope is sincerely that someone will read this text and make better decisions than I made along the way, or see things for what they are sooner than I did.

A NOTE REGARDING ALL THAT IS TAYLOR SWIFT

As I set out to write about my past romantic entanglements, it became an impossibility to ignore the lyrics running through my head as I typed out my story. Taylor Swift's music has been something I've appreciated since her career first began! What I didn't have much knowledge of when I first started writing is copyright laws and the rules regarding typing out lyrics of a music artist when you're writing a book. So I just kept writing out my story, realizing there were song titles and lyrics that fit the story **all too well** to not be included along the way…

Taylor Swift's music has gotten me through the break-ups I wrote about in this book. Taylor Swift was by my side as I made mistakes, fell in love, had my heart broken, and picked myself back up and started dating again. She allows millions of fans to be by her side, feeling what she's been through in romantic endeavors, all set to the tune of her amazing music. So it makes sense that as I recalled the ups and downs of my dating life, her words would be playing through my head…

It came to my attention that using lyrics in this book could potentially be a copyright issue. As such, I began looking into "how to contact Taylor Swift" – and I reached out accordingly. I haven't heard anything back from the emails I wrote to her record label, nor has Taylor herself written back via Instagram (although she's busy overseas on the **Era's Tour** so I get it…). While I've never met Taylor in person, I'd like to think I know her well enough to say the following: Taylor Swift would never want to stifle someone else's creativity. Call this my best attempt at **trying to know somebody** I've **never met**, but I have to believe that's the case.

I doubt I'll ever hear back from Taylor's camp. But she's written about just about any romantic complication someone can go through – and if you haven't found a song that fits your own personal experience, just wait for her next album to drop 😊. That being said, anyone with a direct line to Miss Swift, see if you can get her to sign something guaranteeing she won't sue me. 😊

*I have a second book in which I explain exactly how Taylor came to be incorporated into these pages…It's a funny story involving my kickball team. We shall see if it comes to print – and if it does, it's called **Closure**.

TOTAL TANGENT TIME #2…

I had a friend beta read the first 40 pages - a friend that was not previously into Taylor's music – and not only was she eager to read the rest of the book, but I believe I just turned her into a Swiftie as well! She's going through an emotional divorce, and so I provided her with the following list (as my friend inquired, "aren't most of her songs about break-ups?" I said "…not exclusively…" But then I made her this list…lol)

When you're feeling nostalgic about the relationship…
Red
All Too Well (the 10 minute version if you wanna feel all the feelings)

When you miss him…
Last Kiss
Back to December
I almost do

When you're over it / moving forward…
Bye-bye baby
I forgot that you existed
Clean
Begin Again

When you're pissed off he's a fucktard...
Picture to burn
We are never getting back together
Forever and Always
Mean

When you just wanna blame him...
A perfectly good heart
White horse
Cold as you
Better man
You're not sorry
Mr. Perfectly Fine

When you know you need to move on but you're still sad...
Breathe
We were happy

    The greatest gift I can give someone I care about is an opportunity to heal their heart by introducing them to an artist who has helped me time and again to heal my own. So, to my friend, I hope you found this list helpful. And to Taylor Swift, thank you for <u>everything</u>. My best friend, Britt, is flying into town to see "The Eras Tour" movie with me in a few weeks, on opening weekend. In the very slim chance Queen T ever reads these words, keep making the whole world **shimmer!**

    Lots of love to anyone who read this far! Xoxo

ABOUT THE AUTHOR

Bruce Langdon is a first-time author excited to (over)share with the world about romantic endeavors and their highlights, including true love, major mistakes, breakdowns in communication, and all the bumps and bruises along the way. Bruce moved to North Carolina from Atlanta to start college as a young gay man. Life was bound to be riddled with lessons learned, and now as a grown-up adult and full-time therapist, reflecting on these lessons proves to be an eye-opening and entertaining love story.

www.ingramcontent.com/pod-product-compliance
Lightning Source LLC
LaVergne TN
LVHW041701060526
838201LV00043B/527